Witness

*A true story of addiction,
redemption, & faith:*

*one man's testimony
to the work
of God
within him.*

Lee W. Hollingsworth

InService Press, LLC

Published by InService Press, LLC, 515 East Crossville Road, Suite 420, Roswell, GA 30075, USA

International Standard Book Number:

978-0-615-24907-0

Printed in the United States of America

Quantities of this book are available with special discounted bulk pricing to facilitate fundraising and distribution by humanitarian, spiritual, religious, charitable, educational and other non-profit service organizations.

The author is committed to assist and support such efforts as he is able, including personal appearances, workshops, readings, and talks that may help good causes.

www.leehollingsworth.com

Contact: lee@leehollingsworth.com

Back cover summary written by W.E.B. Griffin.
Cover Design by Robbie Hunt. Photography by John Watson.

Witness

Preface

Like most addicts and alcoholics, I slowly withdrew from everyone and everything, into a shrinking cocoon of me and my poison.

When nothing else matters but the drugs, even life itself, you live in a suspended haze without clocks, laws, health, or other people—unless they have something you need. People are no longer a pleasure; they are simply one of two things: a vehicle to obtain chemicals, or a nuisance to be avoided. Of course, police fall vividly into the nuisance category, but so do loved ones eventually. Their loving pleas to change, to quit, to save yourself are silly, melodramatic, and monotonous. Conversations distill to one topic–when are you going to get help?

My behavior had grown more bizarre in public. Police arrived to check me out for no obvious reason. To me, I was perfectly normal. What was so wrong with banging on a guitar all night in the hospital when my wife was giving birth and I was too loaded to play a lick?

Organized groups become a nuisance, so you stop participating. They have schedules. They meet at a certain time and place. *Boring.* My denial had quickly twisted my inability to show up anywhere on time into an achievement. I had achieved what every one else in the world so desperately wanted. I was able to go wherever I wanted, whenever I wanted. The fact was, I couldn't get anywhere. I couldn't plan to be at a certain place at a certain time unless it involved drugs. But my denial told me I was *free.* I was living the American dream.

What a jerk.

Money had allowed me to perpetuate and extend these myths for years. My long labor to develop my own business was eventually rewarded. My manipulative skills were honed by the graduate school of addiction. The cash told me I had found success. I congratulated myself generously. I was a genius, a gift to mankind that everyone else was just too stupid to see. Morons. It was all about me. How I had managed to run a business at that time remains one of the great unanswered questions of science.

As with all developing addicts, I didn't tend to gather friends and admirers. In fact, I had insulted and horrified those I did have. Relationships deteriorated and were vacated. I was alone with my ego, my denial, my drugs, and my insanity.

At my first day in rehab, I was told that group activities and therapy were a central part of each patient's day. I hated to burst their bubble, but I told them I wanted nothing to do with groups and deserved private, individual therapy. With a confident smirk I said, "Don't worry, I can pay for it."

They looked at me quizzically and gave each other a knowing smile without interrupting their activity.

Was I in for a surprise.

Chapter One

Insanity

The first thing I always noticed was a noise in another part of the house. When my body had finally collapsed at the end of another drunken, drug-filled debauch, there was a certain dead weight that gravity assigned to it. I could be down for days, always fully clothed, and never in a bed. My body gave out and I would lie where I fell. At some point my senses would begin to return, slowly, one by one. The stiff awareness of a searing pain usually came first, followed by the wretched cling of sweat drenched clothes and the stale disgust of long gone alcohol.

Coming to, my eyes still caked shut, I would hear a noise somewhere in our enormous house, a bump, the sound of the kids coming in, a doorbell or the telephone, something to coax me into the here and now. After a roaring binge, and the face-down-in-the-carpet coma that would always follow, consciousness dawned slowly. I could have been on the floor twenty hours or more. The last year of my using I never once made it to bed and stayed there. I always passed out on the floor, a chair, the sofa, whatever. I went and went and went until my body and mind shut down. Deliberately go to sleep? That had become a foreign concept.

Reality set in. I wouldn't dare look up, and I usually had no idea where I was. I figured out I was coming to. Then came the anxiety, the rush of fear, guilt, and dread, as I would try to piece together the previous night.

I cracked open one eye into the fibers of the carpet. On the floor, face down next to the bed, I had a rat's eye view of the entire room. The bathroom door was ajar. Someone pleasantly hummed, probably my wife putting up fresh towels. I didn't need to see her right now. Playing dead was the easiest thing to do.

It was a typical hot, Georgia summer. Along with a dry mouth and parched throat, my head ached. My nose felt stuffed and heavy. I dared not move a muscle because every inch of my body throbbed in pain. I didn't have the courage to open the other eye. I could see on the other side of the bed my wife's footsteps going back and forth as she tended to her day. Man, did I ache! Just another minute. Please. Finally, she left the room. I couldn't face the rebuke I was due. Even worse, I couldn't face the pained resignation that lined her face. All of the times she had protested, fought, cried, and prayed had come to naught.

"Why are you doing this to us? Why would you endanger your children? Why would you endanger yourself? What did we ever do to deserve this? Where is

the man I married?"

He was committing felonies and slow, sure suicide all the while thinking he was doing great. Pure insanity.

In 1996 I bought my family a large house to show I was a great dad and husband. Of course, I never bothered to ask my wife or kids whether they even wanted this house or the neighborhood. I liked it—big, impressive, prestigious, Roswell riverfront.

As a 42-year-old, married father of three young children, one would think I would buy a house compatible with the needs of my growing family. Nope. I liked it, and that was all that mattered. One might also think it was unusual for a successful businessman to be driven to the closing by his real estate agent because he was too loaded to drive himself. Nope. That was me, family man, a success, Mr. Big Deal, Mr. Class. Ha!

There I was, face down in the rank carpet. My nose was crushed in the dirty weave. Grits of sand and God knows what else caked my forehead and chin. My arms lay lifeless. It was hot. Where was I? Are there any bones broken?

I needed a hint of orientation to prepare me for whatever terror would confront me when I rose. I didn't want to see my wife at that moment. Maybe I could propel myself across the carpet moving only my feet. I didn't want to move, but it was inevitable.

Memory drifts in slowly. The bathroom was only

fifteen feet away. If I could get there before anyone
interfered....

Slowly, without raising my throbbing head off the
floor, I dragged myself to the bathroom inch by inch. I
pulled my head up to sink level and splashed water on my
crusty, filthy face. The water burned my raw hands.

My nose felt like a garbage disposal laid low by the
industrial volumes put through it the night before. A three
way dam of chemicals, mucus, and swollen tissue from all
the straws, paper, drugs, and abuse heaped up it. During
my unconsciousness, it had dried into a rock hard
monument to heavy, serious partying.

My only concern now was how I could get more
drugs up it. But this wasn't a new problem. It had become
the most common and certainly the most powerful concern
in my life. And I had become good at it. I even took
perverse pride in my ability to obtain drugs while in
complete denial about the heavy cost I accrued.

A quick shower would loosen the clogs, or maybe
just soaking my head under a faucet if I couldn't make the
shower. I only needed a few grains to pass through. That
would clear me for the truckload to follow, and a victory for
my personal pleasure would be scored, pushing reality back
into the cave where it belonged.

I pulled my head up to the sink, one arm pulling,
the other pushing. I ran the water across my face, soaking
my head in a full basin of water. Toweling off, I was close to

my renewal.

After crushing pills into a magic powdered potion of Ritalin, cocaine, Percodan, and Valium, I stretched out a long fat line of powder next to the sink. Rolling up a dollar bill, I crammed it into my aching, bleeding nose and gave a hearty snort that took up all the powder in a mighty force.

My nose cleared, the powder rushed up, and my brain jumped for joy. My body straightened and my aches and guilt fell away to what had become my mighty protector, guardian, friend, business partner, and family.

I was on top of the world. I was livin' the <u>dream,</u> baby! Yeah! All better now. What was I so worried about, anyway? Thank God I could think ahead and have plenty on hand.

"Honey? How are you? The house looks great! You are great! Where are the kids? I think I have it all figured out at work. Let me see ya, Baby! What a great day, isn't it?"

I bet everyone wished they could be me.

Chapter Two

Beginnings

It wasn't like I started out to be an alcoholic or a drug addict, but I sure enjoyed the fun that alcohol and drugs seemed to create.

My friends and I grew up in a magical, heady time for youth where fun seemed to be everywhere. In 1964 I was ten years old. We all rushed home from Church that Sunday night to see the Beatles perform on Ed Sullivan. Rock 'n Roll was one of the first great discoveries we made as kids long before our parents knew what was going on. Color TVs replaced black & white and the world came alive. Air conditioning came into its own, while surfing and cars were the "fun, fun, fun" the Beach Boys sang about. Skateboards made us look cool, and my friend, Jim, had just gotten a new Honda 125 motorcycle. Girls went through puberty like a magnificent present from God. Except for the omnipresent parental control and our constant lack of money, it was a glorious era.

Stealing sips of whiskey in our parents' boathouses, or sneaking it along on Boy Scout trips was just cool. Waking up in a vomit-filled sleeping bag wasn't, but hey, we could take it. Our hedonistic quest had begun, and it wasn't for amateurs.

When I turned sixteen in 1970, we were a full-fledged movement. We rationalized our disdain for work with a cloak of politically respectable non-conformism. This was ironic, since we were extremely conformist within ourselves and bowed to peer pressure readily. We discovered many new concepts that our parents were way too dense to ever understand. War was bad, art and music were cool, you could think independently and not be struck by lightning, and so on. The pill was a generational Godsend. We guys still couldn't quite duplicate the Hugh Hefner/James Bond girl slaying phenomenon, but we sure tried.

Anyone with long hair was sophisticated, especially if he played a musical instrument or had hitchhiked farther than the county line. Those who were in possession of or had tried drugs were simply exotic. We thought we were the first to discover the wonders of marijuana, beer, and LSD, and we could do illegal acts and not get caught, or hardly ever. The "establishment" was wrong about everything. Their silly laws served no purpose but to keep us from having fun. Why should we have to obey? All it took was courage to ignore their obsolete and pointless rules. Our parents weren't as worldly and smart as we were about such matters, as we endlessly tried to explain to them.

Sunny Florida was a great place to grow up. In the 50's and 60's North Florida was a sultry extension of South Georgia. The real Florida started about 100 miles south, where the oaks and Spanish moss gave way to scrub brush, oyster shells, and sun-lotioned girls in halter tops.

My Dad grew up in northwest Georgia, my mother in Americus, Georgia. They met when my mother attended Shorter College in Rome, in the late forties, and were married in 1952. Mom studied religion at Shorter, maybe because Grandpa Joyner was a Disciples of Christ minister. He died in 1959 when I was five, but I can still remember the thrill of the old fedora he let me wear when visiting, and the pocket watch he carried in his vest, just like railroad conductors in old movies. I remember him as a gracious and stately man. I wish I could have known him better.

After my grandfather's death, my grandmother continued to live in the house my mother grew up in at Taylor Street and Horne. Almost every summer I would travel from Jacksonville to rural Americus to spend six or seven weeks with my grandmother. This wonderful ritual began about 1964 and pretty much ended when I was about sixteen or so, when driving and dating made me way too cool to endure the rigid structure my grandmother revered.

She got on my nerves. It is only now that I can imagine what a pain I was during that time.

In those summers I became acquainted with many of those whom I know to this day. My cousin Ricky was two weeks my senior, and his family came into enough good fortune to afford one of the first color TVs in town! Color was magical. We all thought it was something Disney and Bonanza had invented. Americus was a small south Georgia town with one theater, and if you didn't see someone during the day, you could probably catch them at the Martin Theater that night, enjoying the latest Pink Panther or Elvis Presley movie.

All of the kids in the town liked to congregate at the miniature golf course when not at the Martin Theater. I met many friends there, engaged in many junior high school flirtations, and at the tender age of thirteen, met my future wife, and definitely my mortal savior, Emily Sheffield. She was ten at the time. While we didn't even date until ten weeks before we were married seventeen years later, I did steal my first kiss from her in that time. Unfortunately for me, I had better things to do and see. But eventually, God brought me back to Americus and provided me with one of the greatest gifts a man could have. I don't deserve her.

My grandmother was stern, and it annoyed me to no end. As I look back now, I see the much broader picture. She was dedicated, even hard-headed I guess, to seeing that the small Christian Church on Lee and Taylor Streets would not be neglected under her watch. Her late husband presided there for so many years despite being dwarfed by the next door Methodist and Baptist facilities.

Even though there was never a large congregation or even a regular pastor at times, my grandmother always made sure there were fresh flowers every Sunday and clean linens for Communion. Sundays became an adolescent guy's nightmare of visiting the old people. Every Saturday night decent people were in early. Hadn't they heard of Jimi Hendrix? Or the injustice of the draft and the Vietnam War?

Isn't it amazing how all of those seemingly naïve and uninteresting people in your early years become the objects of an entirely new appreciation as you age?

Take my parents, for example. My being the father of two boys and a girl, I have enjoyed calling my mom to marvel at how she managed to keep her sanity raising us four kids! She always laughed at this respectful gesture.

As youth have been for ages, we were ten feet tall and bulletproof, and thought we knew a whole lot more than our drab, enslaved, and uncool parents. One by one, we indulged in the taboo milestones of the fun, liberating life we dreamed of. This was a monumental time for fun.

In the late '60s and '70s, an entire generation threw off the yoke of conformity that all adolescents feel. This is not new, but we had numbers. The youth of the great Baby Boom reverberated throughout conventional mores and institutions. A vast population of kids got sick and tired of the same crap at the same time.

In fact, based on media coverage (at least the media my pals and I chose), almost all drug users were rich, successful, cool, and got a lot of girls, like the Beatles, the Stones, James Bond, Dean Martin, and Bob Dylan. It became macho to drink a lot, cool to do drugs. The only dark side of this was in the paranoid imaginations of the older generation, who did not have a clue anyway.

The pill became available in 1961, and suddenly the risk of pregnancy, a huge historical deterrent to promiscuity, evaporated. Vast populations enrolled in universities and schools where first time freedom from parental domination and money, fueled the intellectual arrogance that emboldened a generation to cast off the conventional caution to new ideas.

Many of these new ideas were quite ancient. We can remember our parents' idiotic admonition, "I really do understand, but...." We thought we were discovering all of the great new music, the sex, the freedom, the avant-garde, opposition to authority icons, particularly with regard to the Vietnam War. And we watched as our side won, time and again. We gleefully shouted "I told you so", as the Beatles and Led Zeppelin showed they were not just a passing fad, but were changing music forever. That fuddy-duddy Nixon really was a jerk, and we could kick his butt out of office, and those moronic generals in 'Nam couldn't fool us with that "victory right around the corner" crap.

It was our moral duty to fight them. We knew us better than they did, and we resented the mind-control schools and the simple-minded, unenlightened, redneck cops.

Hadn't they read Thoreau? Of course, we had only skimmed through the CliffsNotes ourselves, but civil disobedience was a wonderful concept to rationalize those early beers we stole from the 7-Eleven, the conscientious objection to world injustice, and occasionally puffing a marijuana joint.

It was all non-conformity to us. We didn't distinguish between breaking our parents' rules, the government's rules, or the social rules that suffocated the older generation. They were outmoded and stifled our burgeoning creativity. Rules were meant to be broken. In fact, we celebrated the breaking of rules as an act of individual courage and personal sovereignty. This was the justification for a variety of crimes. Any law that kept us from having fun pooled into this grouping, and we did not have to comply. Why should we suffer because we are more advanced than our legislatures?

To most of us, society's pot laws, sexual mores, and infatuation with material possessions were all examples of a controlling, ignorant older generation keeping us from almost all the really good fun in life.

And *that* meant war.

We, the Baby Boomers, the giant bulge of post-war fertility, had, and is still having, an enormous effect on society. We could feel the power. We went from outcast little children to mainstream controllers of our own destiny. The rock 'n roll thunder from the beer halls of England lit the fires of teenagers in Memphis. And the country blues of Mississippi radiated to the 45 RPM players around the world. We saw each other on the evening news. We stopped an unjust war. We felled an authoritarian president who underestimated our power.

To our parents, the Depression, Roosevelt, and WWII caused a tremendous conservative shift from the reckless frivolity of their parents' generation: The Roaring Twenties, the stock market crash, ruin, widespread suffering, and eventually war. Living through the painful hangover of the twenties, it is no doubt our parents had clear historical motivation to be a little less cavalier with their freedom. And so, they were more conservative. But we were not chained by any of that. Perhaps we were picking up the personal freedom banner last flown in the 1920s. Good times.

We didn't feel bound by mores, convention, and most importantly, laws. This was an excellent way to justify both laziness (e.g., my boss is a control-freak, this kind of work doesn't align itself with my soul, money is just a tool of oppression) and substance abuse, i.e., underage alcohol, excessive drinking, pot, LSD, etc. Almost anything institutional was suspect. Anything conservative, cautious, or that dampened the party was crazy.

Life had not been hard to us yet. We were young and naïve. I was far more concerned with how big I was, not how small. Consequently, the church made no sense to me at all. Christianity was overbearing and restrictive to the worldly and urbane teenage mind. Religion seemed to me a rural, hick phenomenon, generally associated with the uneducated, the bigoted, and the sterile conformity my friends and I disdained.

Chapter Three

Rejecting Religion

As I stated in the previous chapter, my mother was raised in a very Christian household. She was the only child of a Disciples of Christ minister, and majored in religion in college. She was an active member of a Disciples of Christ Church in Jacksonville, and married my father, a Unitarian.

My father's parents were educators. They were an enlightened oasis in the culturally rigid, and often intolerant society of the Deep South of the '30s and '40s. He had a Masters degree and had traveled the world after a near death experience from the business end of a North Korean machine gun in 1951.

I was raised in a liberal religious environment, at least for that time and place. Even so, from my 13-year-old perspective in 1966, I looked at my parents' requirement to go to church on Sunday as the forced Bataan Death March. My totalitarian parents had tyrannical economic power over my budding creativity and growth. My infinite wisdom, maturity, and far superior worldly experience (after all, I understood the Beatles and their importance to the future of mankind) made me far more the wiser in these matters. So at thirteen, I had enough of this BS and stopped taking Communion. It raised a few eyebrows in the sanctuary that Sunday, but I didn't care. I was moving on.

And I did not take Communion again for thirty years.

* * * *

There is something macho in taking almost anything further, longer. As teenagers, guys love to be able to have a story to tell. The ability to recant dangerous, adventuresome stories is extremely cool when you are fourteen. We would spend hours in rapt attention when one of our friends relayed exotic stories of hitchhiking to California, or camping out at Woodstock. Confidently "holding your own" in conversation when gathered before school was important.

I had lots of friends. I was very social and had many acquaintances. There were a few groups I couldn't crack, but I was warmly received in most places. This continued in my early using but evaporated as my usage grew.

By the time I went to college, it was routine to smoke pot every chance I got and could afford. It was especially correct when returning to my hometown for the weekend to reacquaint with old buddies. It was part of the "good life". We generally received good grades, had great girlfriends, and were excited about the future unfolding before us. We had established our own style which seemed to be a huge step up from our conventional parents. They were so cautious, so provincial, so bland, so lifeless. They were the Nurse Ratchets to our McMurphy. We were the emerging underdogs, and we had numbers, huge numbers, and the world changed to suit us. After all the teachers, homework, rules, rules, and more rules, we sure deserved it. Why, we must have been the most deprived and deserving generation ever.

I remember a Swiss exchange student staying in my parents' Jacksonville home whom I met when I was home from Florida State University for a weekend. He and I bunked together in my parents' garage apartment, my high school bachelor pad and generally party central for me and my friends.

He was a great, affable guy with excellent English. We were amazed at how such an educated and worldly dude was so unaware of the beauty of massive alcohol and drug intake. It was as if he had yet to discover something as basic as sex.

We smoked pot all the time, and drank beer from early afternoon every day. He barely participated, even though he sat with us in our party pad and listened to music and talked. This was weird to us. How could you sit around, talk, and listen to music, with massive amounts of drugs and alcohol right in front of you, and not even seem interested. It struck me at the time when he politely, and curiously asked us if we smoked pot like that at university, and we just laughed and laughed. This kid really needed to get out more. He had come to the right place, but it was amazing to us that he had not run into this behavior before, given that everyone was doing it. Little did we know everyone was not doing it!

This also happened with the Argentine exchange students who came in the early seventies, but by that time we didn't really give a damn whether anybody else used or how much.

But when I visited Argentina, wow, did I stand out. Almost no one got drunk, even the young kids. I mean no one. Pot was unheard of. I was the only one who got drunk at parties, and afterwards, even though I would be kidded with good-natured labels like "boracho" (drunk), I didn't care. To me, I had a world to lead in the ways of Bacchus and Eros. It was my duty to bring this weird way of looking at life into the modern world, so they could enjoy this wonderful world of drunkenness.

I remember asking my close Argentine friend, Guillermo, why nobody drank to excess. He responded, "You get nowhere with the girls." Even the simplicity of this global behavioral axiom for men—beware any action that slows your progress with women—did not give me pause to doubt my drunkenness. Asked why no one seems to use illegal drugs, he said "You get nowhere with the girls, <u>and</u> you go to jail." They also knew that the drunker you became, the less luck you were bound to have with the pretty girls. Why start such a critical competition at a disadvantage?

That was true in the U.S., too, but we seemed to get over it. Hey, we were heroes. Argentines, the Swiss, and most everyone else obviously didn't have the same guts, or the same pleasure ambitions, that we had. We were Americans. We could do what we wanted.

As I look back, I have to laugh at myself. If I don't, I might cry.

* * * * * *

My best friend in the world today is that Argentine guy, Dr. Guillermo Gonzalez-Prieto, now a prominent physician in Buenos Aires with three children. He saw my philosophy play out in a most dangerous destructive demise over the many years I've visited his country. He tells me he thought I would die. Many times. He recoiled at my self-induced decline into destruction. Unfortunately, there was nothing the doctor could do except watch my self-destruction from the sidelines and hope for a miracle.

Argentina has always held a magical attraction to me. Maybe it is as simple as knowing great people there.

There is a certain depth that friends and family have that has been forged from the smelter of chaos in their economies, currencies, and government. It is what they depend on.

As a tall, lecherous, blond North American who wore shorts all the time, I definitely stood out. But I didn't care. They drank a lot less than me. I cared even less. My first thought was that it was because they were poorer than we Americans and could not afford to live the life of bliss and plenty that I could. Nope, wrong again.

For some reason, it doesn't occur to drink excessively to the average Argentinean adolescent male, even in the 70's, when drugs and excess seemed de rigueur. This puzzled me. One would think in a country with no drinking age whatsoever, the kids would be absolutely falling down drunk everywhere. But no, it wasn't a big deal to them like it was to us. To them, drinking a fifth of whiskey was something akin to eating a whole stick of butter. One could, but why?

Of course, we hadn't thought it through that well. In the U.S., with all of the rules and age limits and laws, drink became a glamorous, forbidden fruit of adulthood. At a time when looking adult and cool was everything, adolescents here found a way to separate themselves from these restrictive mores and be independent. Until we were twenty-one it was a hidden, secretive event, obtaining and using alcohol and drugs. It was illegal. Not only did this get one used to drinking in secret, but to chugging the surreptitious drink quickly, and growing accustomed to regularly breaking laws.

This was a very bad way to perceive and utilize drugs, including alcohol. In many ways, the laws to restrict alcohol use had the opposite effect which encouraged widespread, gleefully gluttonous imbibing.

South Americans have always welcomed me with grace and affection, a debt I will gladly try to repay but will never achieve.

I visited Argentina for the first time right after I graduated from FSU. My pal, Guillermo, talked me into driving my new 350 Camaro from Jacksonville, Florida to Buenos Aires, a total of six thousand miles.

Because there was no road between Panama and Columbia, I had to ship the car from New Orleans to Cartagena, Colombia, where we flew down to pick it up and followed the Pan-American Highway past three oceans to Buenos Aires. At twenty-two, it was quite an adventure.

What convinced me to go was my acceptance in the Doctoral program in Finance at the prestigious Wharton School of the University of Pennsylvania for the fall of 1977. I couldn't afford to go there on my entry level salary, so the idea of taking a hot car, and selling it for an enormous profit in Argentina was a shot I had to take. Even though I never sold the car, I will never regret that decision.

I did finally make it to Penn, a year after the fact in the fall of 1978. Wow! An urban, northern city and the Ivy League! I was psyched but completely unprepared academically. I had a lot of catching up to do in a ruthless place notorious for eating its own weak links. It was tough. However, I had one skill I could match with the best of them. I could drink all night and get more loaded than any of them. I didn't intend to get a job afterwards, either. Actually, I had no plans. I liked research, so I was at the best place on earth. I didn't know anyone, and, as the weight of the work bore down on me, a loneliness I wouldn't admit to burned in my brain.

At an early student party, I saw Dick, a prep school party animal, who would become my friend, roommate, and general partner in crime. He stood over in a corner, stoned out of his gourd, a cocktail in one hand, and a shit-eating grin I understood. We were instant brothers in a sea of hilarious insanity.

There seemed to be a special élan about drinking in the Ivy League. There was a lot of it. At least I thought so. My wonderful Andover/Yale roommate and I were prodigious consumers, even becoming co-chairmen of the Student Social Committee. This meant we took home all of the unused liquor after all of the parties we threw on the Committee's budget. We were set. We rented a close by apartment and made many, many friends.

While partying was my expertise, in almost everything else I was so far behind. My ego had a giant hole in it, and I was lonely. But I had some ways to make friends. Being from Florida, I could arrange for much of the cocaine we used our second year. I remember snorting up one morning during finals and flying high during an exam. Oh course, I thought I would get extra credit. To my shocked surprise, I barely passed.

Graduating with only a Masters, I let loose on the world. I made some great decisions along the way, the commitment of marriage, for example, although I can't claim the wisdom of understanding the importance of it at the time. Even though my future wife and I were imbibing when we decided to marry, we did go along with a God-sent inkling that was far above the normal noise of my usual self-centeredness and self-absorption. That is one of the teasing facets of developing addiction. You can and do occasionally make a rational decision.

But, in my case, the compulsions and obsessions grew slowly from their dormancy over many years, showing telltale signs that were easily ignored, dismissed, or rationalized by me.

For example, I was the last in my extended family to let go of cigarette smoking. I had tried many times before, and Emily had already quit when she first became pregnant. For me, it took more.

Emily was only two weeks from the due date of our first child and could have gone into labor any minute. We were visiting my parents in Jacksonville when I went on a huge drunk. My parents told me the next day I was never to step into their house again if I ever thought about doing that again. Here I thought I was just having a good time watching the game. Of course, it was in my parents' den, watching a football game with my brother, Emily, and my parents.

I was the only one there who kept his own private ice chest of cold beer at their feet at all times. I pounded beer after beer, got flailing drunk, and no one else even came close. I was in my own world, pontificating loudly on world events, the whole nine yards. One giant ego released from any semblance of civility.

I also chain smoked a couple of packs of cigarettes. The next day I had one helluva hangover, complete with a disgusting trench mouth of cigarettes and beer, and I stunk like a brewery that had burned to the ground. I was so nauseated I couldn't even look at a cigarette. Emily had to drive the six hours back to Atlanta, with me reeling in the back seat, of no use whatsoever, nursing my head and body and trying to sleep off the pain I had brought on myself, by myself.

It was in this misery that I went for two whole days without smoking a cigarette, just because I was so disgusted (and disgusting). It gave me the beachhead to start. I bought some nicotine gum, and before long I had gone two weeks. I drank tons of water and chewed ice, and still do. I haven't overcome that basic hand to mouth reflex. I put something healthy in my hands these days and let it go. I haven't smoked since 1988. But like so many things I have had to let go, there are probably claw marks on that last pack.

So how did I progress from heavy drinking to drugs? Drugs, particularly pills, are easier to hide, and their effects are easier to disguise. My insane logic came up with the brilliant strategy of using drugs instead of alcohol. Even though they were illegal, they were smaller (easier to carry around and use) and more powerful, thus giving me more bang for the buck. The effects weren't as noticeable as the socially repugnant physical inabilities of being blind drunk. I thought myself pretty clever. It was a clever solution that let everybody be happy. Especially me.

The idea of simply drinking less had evaporated slowly. Yes, I told myself many times that I could and would contain it. After a certain number of drinks or a certain time I would stop. But I could never stick to it. When that limit was reached, I always seemed to be having too much fun. Every time I somehow felt it was important to continue this blissful state, I improved on it by more drinking and using. I felt alive, but as everyone but me could clearly see, that ironic feeling of well-being was just an illusion. That wonderful, fun feeling was, in reality, death calling my name. As long as alcohol or drugs were in my system, I went with it, mesmerized in its fatal spell.

Chapter Four

The Downward Spiral

Forming my own business in 1989, I rented office space from a buddy of mine in real estate, Jack Brown. Jack has been a wonderful friend over the years, and still is. I met Jack when Emily and I moved from our Atlanta apartment to the Roswell suburbs in 1988. She was pregnant with John, our first child. Jack lived directly behind us, sharing the rear border of our lots.

Jack and his wife Rita became mentors to Emily and me as we entered the new, unfamiliar, and frightening world of parenthood. With four daughters of their own, and a gregarious and giving nature, we were drawn to them for guidance. Six years my senior, Jack always seemed so adult. I first saw him as President of our neighborhood Homeowner's Association, presiding with calm, cool, dignity. I admired that.

He still is one of the most calming influences in my

life. This impression has solidified as the years have worn on, and I have been privy to the reality of turmoil and challenges that would have rocked a lesser man. Jack freely admits he certainly doesn't feel like a lighthouse of calm and direction, but people who are this way usually don't see it from their own perspective.

Jack ran his business out of an office complex in Atlanta. Having too much space, he rented me an office with its own phone line and allowed me to use his receptionist. Cool. With a few clients at first, I began my business.

During the next three years, I built my business. I had also started having cocaine shipped to me in that ground floor office. Wow! Under the influence, I could sure work hard! And long hours, too. After a while, I would close my office door and spread the drugs on my desk, indulge, and work on the computer, usually till 4 p.m., when the trading day was over. The drugs seemed to make even the most mundane chores fascinating. I would usually find myself still there at 11 p.m., then have to force myself to leave my "play time".

Emily was home with three young kids. This was the beginning of years of late nights and missing days, and after ten years clean, I still have not even approached penitence for this abuse to her and the family.

In 1991-1992, the Internet was just emerging. I knew it would be huge, especially in my investment business where the whole game is fresh information and the analysis of that data. I called what I was doing "research", sort of "free-form research". But it was so disjointed at first that I literally became lost in it all, using stimulants to keep myself exploring this endless new cyber world.

It, and I, had no focus. We were made for each other, and the cocaine and my emerging addiction lit a fire of compulsion and obsession. The Internet did have some legitimacy to it as it became a historic new information venue that would change mankind forever. I was on top of it, and I was finally making money. Even though I would spend time experimenting with wild new languages and protocols and worldwide communications capabilities that might never have a use, it was mainly after hours. As the money grew, our kids entered fine private schools. Everything worked so well. At least, that's the way it seemed to me. But as the isolation grew, I spent more hours awake and found myself meandering in my Mercedes at all hours. I felt no fatigue except when I crashed. And then relief was very, very quick.

To get to my office, I had to walk around to the front of the building, in the front door and past the receptionist. Take a right past the fax room, then a left, and my office was on the right. Now, being on the side of the building, my big office window faced directly onto the parking lot, and I usually parked my car right in front of that window. I thought it pretty clever to exit my office by the window, and not have to take that laborious, convoluted path out by the receptionist. What's so weird about that? I can imagine what people thought of me crawling out of my office window, especially late at night. Interestingly, it also allowed me to avoid seeing other people in the office, but that never really occurred to me. I fully rationalized my increasingly bizarre behavior.

I am both blessed and cursed by the memory of endless strange actions I took while under the influence. Only as I look back now am I incredulous over these episodes, and that I really thought they were a good idea at the time. It constantly reminds me of how twisted a mind can become, and how deep denial and rationalization can make incomprehensible actions seem completely normal.

Here are a few of those things that actually happened, all of which seemed to me at the time to be perfectly logical. I was amazed that the rest of the world had quite a different opinion of them.

Each example probably has some kernel of logical intent, but that sliver of reality is grotesquely deformed by an addict's insane perspective.

House shopping at 4 a.m. (Sandy Springs, GA 1993):
I was loaded to the gills, wide awake, and didn't want to go home. I decided my family deserved a larger house, and that 4 a.m. would be the perfect time to cruise my Mercedes

around wealthy neighborhoods to get a feel for what I might want to buy. My business would surely continue to the stratosphere, and it was high time we had a residence equal to my soon-to-achieve station.

Taking a week's drug stash on a family trip to Disney World (Summer, 1996) with my three young pre-teen kids and my father-in-law:

I slept all day while the wife and her father took the kids to see the sights. Then I went out all night searching for other partiers (newsflash to Lee: at Disney World, there aren't many!).

I decided Disney World would be much more fun without the family, and I sent them home by themselves so I could stay there and really party. What a great son-in-law, huh? I became so unmanageable by myself that I lost my wallet.

Having only my in-resort Disney charge card and no other I.D. or credit card, I couldn't board a plane home. In fact, I couldn't go anywhere off the Disney property. Actually, I could have left, but I was rapidly becoming such a flaming jerk that no one wanted to help me. Finally, the hotel general manager actually assigned a young valet to be my personal escort, to drive me around, collect all of my things, and be sure I got on a plane *outta* there. It took two days. Of course, I thought they were giving me my personal servant because they recognized my status as a VIP. What's so weird about that?

Taking two days for a three hour drive to South Georgia:

Doesn't everyone have to stop occasionally for hallucinations? (1996) One holiday weekend I sent my family ahead to the in-laws lake place so I could finish up some "critical work". Actually, with no one in the house it became my castle. I could really use...ah...I mean work. No interruptions, no kids bursting in, no pesky wife or chores, nothing but delicious isolation with the one I loved. I could use much more freely.

But after hundreds of really annoying phone calls from my wife wondering why I hadn't left yet, I finally dragged my nose out of my briefcase and left on the three hour journey at about 11 p.m., not having slept for three days. Despite the fact I had made this trip hundreds of times, I found myself hopelessly lost in the back roads of rural Georgia by 2 a.m.

Too stupid to stop, I continued the journey until hallucinations of the road rising up and twisting into snakelike shapes of green and yellow scared even me. I pulled into a huge, fallow field about forty miles from my destination. I followed the dirt path down to a dip in the earth so maybe a passing cop wouldn't notice a Navy Mercedes Benz sitting in a stark naked hundred acre field. (What's so weird about that?) I sure didn't want some country cop tapping on my window. As I drive by that spot today, my stomach cringes to see that the place in the field where I had parked was right in front of a farmhouse I hadn't noticed that night.

I passed out until dawn and made the final forty miles. Total time for a three hour drive—two days. (Hey, it happens to everybody, right?)

Never using in front of the kids or my wife, and thinking I kept my insanity a secret, even though I spent all of my time in bathrooms.

Or having the police called on me while:

Getting a haircut (Roswell Hair Salon, 1994):
I went in for a hair cut in the middle of the day, when most people were at work. I had no idea why I tried this new salon, maybe because I hadn't been welcome at most of the others. There were about nine or ten chairs occupied by women customers, all minding their own business or chatting quietly with those they knew.

The salon owner was a very effeminate male, who had parked his enormous lavender truck in the front and proceeded to flit about the shop. No one really paid him any mind except me. I thought this was just hilarious. A gay hair salon owner with a lavender truck. I didn't know him or anyone else in the salon that day, but I naturally assumed everyone thought this was as funny as I did. I felt no pain, having been up the previous night, and was on a huge stimulant buzz. Most people know of a drunk that thinks himself hilarious. Multiply that by ten and you have me that day. Gross misperception is a very typical condition of intoxication. Anyway, I began to taunt and pick at the guy with great confidence my wit would be appreciated by all. It wasn't. Without any encouragement whatsoever, I continued to amuse myself.

It wasn't long before a police car pulled up to the salon. Strange, I thought. Maybe they were coming in for a trim. No chance. A cold shiver went down my spine as fear welled up from my stomach. They came directly toward me. They escorted me out and had me sit on the sidewalk next to my Mercedes. I guess they had never encountered "Styling Under the Influence", but they assured me severely that I would be thrown in jail if I got back in my car. So I didn't. I walked away.

At the time, I thought what a pain these police officers had been. Now I realize what an incredible break they gave me, and how much restraint they truly showed.

In the hospital's maternity waiting room
(Shallowford Hospital, July 1995):

While my wife was in labor with our third child, I stayed in the waiting room. After a few hours, the doctors decided to let my wife sleep for the night and induce labor in the morning. They set up a gurney next to my exhausted wife for the night, but I couldn't sleep. Then I became bored. Luckily, I was prepared for just this situation. Doesn't everyone bring a guitar and ice chest to the hospital and play and sing off-key all night?

Having morning coffee with "the guys" at the corner convenience store:

The trouble was, I had been up on alcohol and stimulants for two days, came in at 7 a.m. to buy beer, and acted like I actually knew some of these hard working people who were just waking up and going to work. They didn't call the cops until after I left (maybe they were in fear of their life), and they gave the police my license tag number. You can't imagine how surprised I was when the police cruiser rolled up to my house an hour later.

They said they wanted to be sure I was off the road, but I knew it was part of a huge international conspiracy to be sure I wasn't having too much fun. Yeah, that was it.

All in all, it was a party that would never end. I was just getting good at this lifestyle. Everyone envied me because I could get away with it and they couldn't. Or so I thought.

But, as everyone knew but me, I was not going to get away with it. They tried to warn me, that I was inviting disaster to my health, freedom, and my life, but I dismissed them. I was way too smart, way too rich, and way too powerful for anything or anyone to even think they could make me do anything against my will.

In truth, I was not rich, I was very stupid, and I was at the weakest point in my life. Soon the vast chasm between what I perceived and what was real, would come to a crashing and painful reconciliation.

Chapter Five

Hope

I couldn't believe I was in the back of a police car.
My 560 SEL Mercedes, parked several feet away, looked at
me helplessly. I wouldn't see that car again for a long time.

The time was about one a.m., June 30, 1997. They
had caught me red-handed. Not only was I high as a kite
and my disheveled car full of all kinds of illegal pills, but
they also confiscated the actual forged prescription I'd just
tried to fill. I saw them put it in a plastic bag for evidence.

I was caught.

Even so, I still thought I could talk the cop driving
me to jail into letting me go. My persuasion centered on
convincing him that by booking me, he would actually
create a criminal. In my strange rationale, I had not
actually been a criminal until I was caught. And then, only
when it came out in public. To me, it was this policeman's
fault. I was the victim. By not letting me go, he would ruin
my family's life and create a low class, unemployable felon.

What a childish mindset I had! If no one saw it, it didn't exist. These were unjust, silly laws anyway, meant to contain the little people who had to steal to buy drugs. I didn't need anybody. I was productive. Everybody who was anybody made money. This short-sighted policeman was blind to this entire concept. As I tried and tried to explain to him on the way to jail, in my endearing and persuasive slur, he seemed to act like he had heard it all before. But I had to make him understand before it was too late and I was actually booked into jail.

Certainly, he didn't realize who I was. He interrupted every once in a while only to suggest that I might get "help." I had no earthly idea what he was talking about.

"But officer" went my lament as we cruised to the station house, "if you take me in, it will only make me a criminal. There is no coming back. Do you really want that on your conscience?" I tried everything. He surely had never met such an upscale and clever guy who deserved a break.

No luck. Jail. Two a.m. now. I stood in front of the sergeant's desk as he filled out a form and held the fake prescription I had brought into the pharmacy.

This did not look good.

He didn't smile. He placed the paper in a Ziplock bag and ordered me into a holding cell across from his mammoth desk while he finished the processing.

Miserable, I wondered how I could explain this to Emily. There was no way I could get out of jail, get my car, and get home before she woke up to prepare the kids for school. What a disaster! I knew I'd have to call her. I also needed to call an attorney. Three a.m. now.

My friend, Jerry, owed me. He was a general attorney and lived far away from my town of Roswell. That was important. I didn't want anyone in my town to discover what a low life I'd become. After all, I had an image to protect. Yes, that was the most important thing. People thought I was a genius, and they were right, too. This was just one of the tough breaks all great achievers had to go through once in a while. The road to greatness is tough! Unbeknownst to me, most of my community knew me far better than I gave them credit for. I never even wondered why neighborhood parents would rarely let their kids come inside our house.

So what would happen to me? This is the kind of thing that makes the newspapers. I was locked up tight for a huge felony, with jailers that could care less. Panic started to set in. What would happen? What would I do?

Wait a minute, what was that I felt in my sock? Could it be? Was that...so familiar...was my mind playing tricks? I slowly checked with my fingers being sure the cops outside couldn't see me. Yes, it is! One last capsule of Oxycodone! Oh, blessed relief! There is a God!

As I managed to slyly slide that slick red capsule in

my mouth, the only thing I could think of was my good fortune. Filthy, disgusting, and sitting in a jail cell with my poor family at home not yet knowing what Dad had gotten himself into, and all I could think about was the next hour of personal pleasure some big red capsule would provide, and to hell with what would happen after.

All too soon, the pleasure was over. I was in a slow train wreck of bad dreams that all happened to be real. Now I had to make that three a.m. phone call to my frantic, innocent wife, at home with three small ones, praying for me. It was awful, trust me. Don't ever let yourself get in that situation.

Next came the four a.m. call to my attorney, a strip search, a strip shower, and jail issue garb, ill fitting and grimy. Like me.

Just when I thought I knew the full extent of feeling bad, I came off that last high full-force into the harsh reality of jail. The physical toll on my body, the years of grinding hyperactivity and no sleep rushed forth in a torrent of bone sapping fatigue. There was no place to hide, no place to rest.

The drunk tank was a cold, stainless steel basin with a giant sink, complete with a drain at one end to wash out the grime, and an open steel toilet at the other. I collapsed on the floor, the metal cool to my sweat baked cheek. The simmering stench of a Georgia July hung heavy in the air. The oily stubble on my face matched the dirty tangles of my hair. My head pounded from a year long amphetamine binge and the agony of opiate withdrawals. Although I hadn't slept for many days, I was in too much physical turmoil to slumber now. So the zombie-like wakefulness persisted. I laid my head in my arms pretending to be dead or insane in the hopes that the rest of the refuse hauled into the tank that night might leave me alone.

Every hour I looked up to see only a minute had gone by. I ached. There was no place to be comfortable. Time passed in slow seconds of misery. Everyone stunk and everyone was stupid. What was I doing here? I guess all great men have their crosses to bear.

I was scared. These were some rough colleagues, all in surly moods I wanted no part of. I put my head down into my arms, avoided eye contact, and moaned in a weird, insane cadence. I wanted to be seen as more trouble than I was worth. Imagine that!

When my wife finally came to bail me out, it was the afternoon of the following day. A long time friend of hers came to support her. I am still grateful to the two of them for coming. Emily wanted to be sure I had no chance of talking her out of going straight to a rehabilitation facility, Ridgeview Institute, located across town. That was her condition for my release—straight to rehab. She had packed my bags. I didn't argue.

The first few days were spent in a locked facility of about twenty beds, with an open central room and nurses' station. It was a closed building, heavily secured, and very difficult to get in or out.

This is where intoxicated patients were brought to detoxify from whatever they had in their system. It was a place to go through withdrawals and maybe survive. Detox usually lasts two to five days, which are, by definition, intense.

The staff never knows what addicts will do as the drugs are being extracted. They have seen it all, the wailings of the psychotic, the ache and misery of withdrawals, and the silence of the unconscious. Nothing is natural, and none of it is pleasant. But that is where everyone has to start.

I shouldn't have been surprised that my fellow patients were in rough shape. This was not my week. This was not my year. To me, the staff stood in stark contrast, clean, well-pressed, and usually in a pleasant, professional mood. The staff also seemed so organized with papers, schedules, and routine. I immediately imagined what pitifully boring lives they must lead. Yes, I was that judgmental. In fact, all of those people saw me exactly for what I was, a gutter level drug addict.

I didn't see myself like that at all. I thought they had never seen anyone so smart, so sophisticated. But they had seen ten thousand versions of me, all with the same disease that was practically impossible to see from the inside.

In rehab, I gradually began to earn privileges. In

the beginning, they won't let you do anything out of their sight. They even came in my little room when I was asleep to check on me every fifteen minutes. They took my vital signs every couple of hours. I thought they were being melodramatic. Not until much later did I realize what a life or death deal addiction is. I was in complete denial.

When the drugs wore off, I ached severely and just wanted to sleep. It seemed like I hadn't slept in years. I had no biological clock, and they always awakened me for group therapy or some other psycho-babble activity.

After a few long days in the detox facility, I was assigned a room with two roommates in the halfway house next door, still within the Ridgeview campus. We were not locked in, but there were a lot of rules that governed our behavior. For example, I had to walk everywhere with a designated buddy until I'd earned the right to walk alone. This promotion, like all decisions, was made in a joint community meeting, with me having to make a request and a case for it, and everyone voting on it. Also, everyone was encouraged to confront each other when anything was amiss. For me, who was used to making my own rules and answering to no one, this was pure hell. But, I persevered. I knew by now that my only chance of avoiding prison was to successfully complete the Ridgeview program and have them advocate to the court on my behalf. So I put my nose to the grindstone with the absolute best intentions of getting clean. Maybe not forever, but certainly long enough to get out of there, and to get my legal troubles behind me.

After about three weeks in Ridgeview my lawyer called me with some bad news. The police had decided to pull up the drug records of all the local pharmacies to determine the extent of my prescription-passing activities. It was a lot. I had been working a variety of pharmacies for years, carefully keeping records so that I would never have to visit the same one more than once a month. As the investigators kept looking, the evidence kept mounting. I had acquired such a large volume of drugs, they began to think I was reselling them, which put an entirely different, and more serious, light on it all. Had they stumbled onto a drug ring? Actually, no, they hadn't. It was only me obtaining massive amounts for personal use. But they didn't learn that until much later. What my lawyer called to tell me was that they increased the charges to seventeen felony charges of forgery. Seventeen felonies.

I knew I had to stay in Rehab and get clean. I had to do exactly as I was told and earn their respect and advocacy. But thinking it and doing it were two different things. At one point I was scheduled to get a much needed weekend at home with my family. I had to be good, to obey all the rules, or the consequences were that I would have to stay at the halfway house. I hated consequences.

I missed my family far more than I thought I would. The first time they came to visit, after I had been there about two weeks, I was waiting in the parking lot as they pulled in. It was wonderful to see my wife's shining, beaming face in the driver's seat, with my older two kids, Katherine and Clayton, happily looking out for me from the side window. But I will never forget the face of my two-year-old, Langdon. I didn't know if he would recognize me. But without hesitation, when he caught sight of me, his arms flung open wide, and he came running at full speed right to me. It was the happiest, most excited and loving look I have ever seen. I'll never forget that innocent love that I had been throwing away with both hands in active addiction.

This was the same young man who just spoke in front of fifty people at my ten year clean anniversary, now twelve years old. How different his life has been with a sober Dad versus the megalomaniac that would have ripped his childhood into shreds of embarrassment, depravity, and despair. There is no greater gift I could have, but you couldn't have explained that to me then. It just wouldn't register.

After sixty days in rehab, trying my best to do what was required, and knowing that to use again was to blow it big time, I was released from Ridgeview. The staff and my doctor had severe reservations, but I convinced my wife to persuade them.

I had to get out of that place. Tax filings were due. In my ego's view, I was essential. To celebrate my release, I bought myself a red Ferrari. My wife and father were appalled, and I had no idea why they thought this insane. The danger that I was one small slip-up away from prison didn't seem to matter. I could see all my problems shrinking in my rear view mirror. And my ego told me I was back in charge. But I had not learned enough. Overconfident at being out and free, my complacency lulled me back into the darkness. After only two weeks out, I relapsed.

Once I started down that line of thought, I quickly concluded that I might as well do it sooner rather than later. I was hurting and aching and sleeping all the time. I was a 17-year-old that had landed in a 43-year-old's body, out of shape and dragged through ten years of abuse. And I knew a way to fix all of that hurt in thirty seconds.

My obsession took over.

Eventually, I figured that the way I would relapse would be to encounter a pill in the house somewhere, even though Emily and some dear friends of hers had frantically tried to clean out everything. It was a big house. I had stuffed drugs in every crevice, so I knew they could not have found them all. I decided, since I would no doubt run across something anyway, I might as well get some relief now, and just go find it. What a thinker.

It didn't take long to find one of those shiny red Tylox capsules hidden in a box of red push pins. Was I a genius or what? I spilled out the white powder and snorted it up my nose. Wow, that was good. I was off to the races.

Soon I couldn't find anymore, and I was really missing the stimulant side of my preferred drug mix, Ritalin. It wasn't long before I had parked my Cadillac in front of an out-of-the-way pharmacy with a freshly forged script in my hand. I would surely go to prison if I was caught, I thought to myself nervously. What would the pharmacist do? Would they throw up their hands in disgust and call the police, or my doctor, or anyone? What if I acted nervous? Hell, I was nervous. What was I *doing* there?

And then my addiction spoke. What if they didn't do anything? Blessed, blessed relief.

Addiction always won this battle for my soul. No matter how long I sat in that car, no matter how much I told myself how bad the consequences could be, addiction always won.

I summoned up my courage, my game face, and with the script in hand, went inside. To be caught was to go straight to prison. I did it anyway. I had truly lost all control.

I did exactly what I did not want to do. I couldn't stop. The enormity of my problem was starting to sink in.

When I started with one drug, it wasn't long before I yearned for my favorite combination of drugs, which required more risky trips to the pharmacy. No matter the risk, I did it anyway.

Once the stimulants were in my system, I locked myself back in my office with the excuse I was doing our taxes. I stayed up all night and came home in the morning. My wife was not amused. I told her I had to finish the taxes, and all the records were in my office, and blah, blah, blah. She looked at me in disbelief. "You relapsed!" I couldn't believe she was so upset.

Even though I had follow-up therapy sessions twice a week, plus she and I had couples counseling another two times a week, I somehow thought I could bluff and lie my way through all of it.

Before I knew it, she came into the room with the phone in her hand, demanding I talk to my doctor, who also happened to be the head of Ridgeview's medical staff. I needed time to figure out how to handle him. Unfortunately, she gave me no time. "He's on the phone, here," she said decisively, shoving the phone to my ear.

The doctor asked how I was, then asked if I had stayed up all night. I said yes. I tried to be calm and natural, as if everybody with important matters stayed up for days and nights. "You need to come in and be drug-tested," he said. That wouldn't be good at all. If they tested me, they would lock me back up. I told him I would be right there, with no intention of doing so. A few hours later I called his office and left a message that I was leaving for Florida and was not telling anyone where I was going. I also said I might leave the country just to throw them off. Then I got in my car and drove five miles to an upscale commercial area of Atlanta and checked myself into a luxury hotel. And started to do drugs.

I pulled out the Yellow Pages and turned to the listings for attorneys. It was five p.m. on a Friday night and I only got recordings. I was obsessed. The more drugs I snorted, the more convinced I was that any attorney would love to have my case, and would look out for things while I jetted off to the Caribbean or somewhere exotic. My mind was so sick that it had twisted the image of drug use and deserting my beautiful, loving family into something both glamorous and noble. Of course, I would send them money, and bring them down for luxury vacations in my fantasy hide-a-way. I was crazy. I didn't even have the decency to tell my wife where I was, or even if I was alive. I thought my doctor would send out a search party if he knew I was in the state. I was so arrogant. He didn't do anything, nor would he. Little did I know that what I thought was my own unique behavior was classic, undeniable addiction. Nobody can make an addict want life.

Over a week's time, I did nothing but use drugs and commit crimes to get them. A friend from rehab finally convinced me to come up to his lake house, which took me about five hours to make a one hour trip. He slowly began to convince me to go back to Ridgeview. After a long time denying that I needed help, I relented. I went home and spent a last night with my family. The next morning my wife took me to Ridgeview. I went in and confessed.

From there I went back to the detox facility where I

had started my journey three months earlier. One of the staff therapists welcomed me back with a warm "we worried about you, and we're glad you made it back alive." What an alarmist, I thought.

It was September 25, 1997, my first day clean, and it was miserable.

I had been through the drill three months before. Everyone remembered me. But I was shocked when the staff told me I would not be allowed back in for treatment. What? Not allowed in? That was ridiculous. I knew of people who had gone through treatment six or seven times. People without money. I had money, brains, and sophistication. What did they mean, no? I couldn't believe it. But they were serious. Detox only, then out.

At first, I wouldn't accept it. After all, I needed Ridgeview to tell the judge what an excellent patient I'd been and that my future was bright. They needed to attest that I was rehabilitated, and prison was not only unnecessary, it would be a detriment to both me and society. I had it all worked out. All I had to do was talk to my attorney. I had gobs of money. He would fix it.

You can imagine how I felt when he said to me, "Hey, Lee, I'm not a magician. I told you to follow their directions exactly, and you might have a chance. You didn't." My heart, my brain, and my bones sank.

I pulled up my chair to the only pay phone, searching the phone book for another rehab facility that would take me and do what I needed. Frantically, I began to dial one after the other. And I prayed. I didn't know how, but I asked for relief and for someone or something to be with me. I felt utterly, utterly alone, locked away from the world, having to ask permission of a lowly staffer just to go to the lunchroom, not to mention the bathroom.

An image came to me of a gerbil in an iron pipe, greased on the inside, the animal furiously clawing against the oily sides. Try as it might, it slowly slipped backward. Try harder! No luck. It was losing the battle. I was losing the battle. I had nothing left. No other treatment center would be any different from this one. The music I had to face was the same tune everywhere. There was no escape. *Father, I can go no further. I have no more hope. I am at the end of the road. I give.*

My wife finally convinced my doctor to continue my treatment on a two week trial basis. If I could make it for two weeks, he would agree to treat me for an additional two weeks, and so on.

And so began my journey back from Hell. No trumpets, no bells, no glamour, nothing. Just emptiness, hopelessness, and surrender. Defeat. And yet, it was my greatest moment of victory. Nothing felt particularly different except that I was still. I was tired and I could rest. My wife had told me many times that I should not have an opinion on anything for a long while. Okay, I would do nothing. I wouldn't think. I would just do as I was told, and pray.

The second day, they allowed me to actually walk down the hall to the lunchroom. This was a big privilege. During those first few days in detox, all patients had to have their meals brought to them. Behavior of new arrivals can be bizarre. Only after the staff felt you could walk down the hall without injuring yourself or others, or wouldn't try to escape, would you be allowed to do so. I had to admit a little pride when they first let me walk down the hall.

I still hurt physically and was exhausted all the time. The staff had this annoying practice of waking me and forcing me to go to group therapy, which I hated. Leave me alone! No way. But I no longer ran the show.

Each day was hard, but it slowly dawned on me that the world, and my life, had stopped getting worse. It seemed like only ninety people yelled at me as opposed to the hundred the day before. And nothing would ever be as bad as that first day.

I hadn't noticed life getting better, even microscopically, for a long while. The best way for things to improve was for me to do nothing. Me! Master of universe, self-made millionaire, father, and husband extraordinaire.

The humiliating truth began to sink in. I was a far lesser man than I thought. I was, in fact, a hopeless mess. Prison was certainly in store, and my beautiful wife and kids were due for a long, long spate of suffering that I caused and was powerless to prevent.

My life had become completely unmanageable. But, as bad as it seemed, therein lay my salvation. There was no way out. I could not be saved by anything I could see, understand, or imagine, and I was scared. The only thing I could do was pray. They told me to pray, so I did. I didn't know how, or what to ask for, but I did it anyway. I prayed to know God and for the willingness to do whatever I needed to do. And it was quiet.

Many don't make it to this point. Or don't stay there. I made some friends and began going to recovery meetings. They said to go to ninety meetings in ninety days. Whew, that seemed like a lot, but I did it because they said to. I asked a friend's sponsor to be mine, and he agreed. Would he be cruel? The thought terrified me, but I did it anyway. He told me to call him every day. I hated calling, but I did that, too. I had no choice.

I had to accept the slowly dawning truth that I might be wrong about everything. I was dealing with more than just prison. This was life or death stuff, and the more I went to meetings, the more I began to learn about addiction and the tragedies that follow it, i.e., divorce, death, broken cars, limbs, and dreams, childhood horrors, abuse, and terror. Degradation and scandal and disgust.

It began to make an impression. I made a buddy named Howard, who was funny, and very interesting. As we hung around together, he made it acceptable to take recovery seriously. For this alone I will always be in his debt. His younger brother, Dave, also came into our circle, and I cannot explain what a difference it made to have friends in the program of recovery. We even chided each other to keep working on the steps, which ended up being life-saving, but seemed light-hearted stuff at the time. There are a lot of very important things that must happen in recovery that usually don't make sense to addicts until a long time after. You have to give up control and follow directions, or you die.

There was also mention of a "higher power". As in Step 2, I came to believe that a higher power could return me to sanity. Like many, I had rejected organized religion as a youth as being beneath me intellectually. They said I didn't have to adopt a higher power, I only had to understand how one could return me to sanity. To do that, I had to understand what a higher power was. Heck, there are tons of things that are more powerful than me. If I'd thought about it, car keys were more powerful, as they could start a car and I could not. The lock on a door certainly was for similar reasons. In fact, almost everything was more powerful. Voila! Truth. And the truth often hurts. I am actually quite, quite small in the scheme of things, and as it began to also dawn on me, most of the things that went on in the universe were not about me at all. It was rarely about me. And it was arrogant and childish to think so much revolved around me.

At thirty days clean I received a silver chip at a

recovery meeting. The Ridgeview staff didn't think I could make two weeks, and here I was at more than four weeks!

A tiny drop of self-esteem came my way. I became familiar with 12-step meetings, and started to actually enjoy the dinners we frequently had afterwards. It wasn't so bad! I knew, however, how fleeting it could be. My wife was wary, as well she should have been. But I began to taste a sweetness I hadn't known in a long time–self-respect. I had never realized that my expanding ego was mutually exclusive to my self-esteem. And that humility is what really gets it back. Weird, no? That is one of the many fascinating paradoxes I had yet to learn and am still discovering.

Chapter Six

Financial Trouble

At this early stage in recovery, I was still naïve. My business continued to do well (meaning the market was doing well which was no reflection on my self-perceived genius). I went where I pleased, did what I wanted. I paid the upscale rehab hospital in cash, about $30,000. For some reason, I felt it beneath me to use insurance. I had coverage; I just didn't want my wonderful permanent record to be sullied by something so plebian. Of course, I ignored the fact my mug shot, arrest record, and the vivid memories of my antics in Florida and Georgia already presented a less than savory image of me and my noble endeavors.

Most people come into the 12 step program as beaten as you have ever seen. The pain of prison, divorce, joblessness, devastation, and ruin are great motivators to make the changes one needs to make. One of the most common denominators is poverty. Many are unemployable, have squandered everything, and frequently don't have enough to throw one dollar in the basket.

For some strange reason (which I know now, but was clueless to then), I was the opposite. I was loaded with money that had come in the fairly recent past. So all of these money problems people whined about were foreign to me. I remember thinking that someone surely must be a schmuck not to have $20,000 lying around in cash to solve whatever problem was at hand. Only $20,000! Hell, I could get that tomorrow. I was a very sick puppy.

No wonder the staff at Ridgeview told me I had almost no chance of staying clean. Even though I had done enough to stay clean to this point, I didn't have a solid foundation when the challenges came. I hadn't developed that gut level desperation to live clean, even though I knew I had to use these tools to solve my massive legal problems. Only a few other "anomalies" and I had money. Driving the Ferrari to meetings didn't help my image, either.

Early on in recovery, I attended an East Cobb County meeting along with Chris C., who had thirteen years clean and actually spoke at one of the Regional Conventions. That made him a giant in my eyes, sort of an old hand at this new, and pretty bizarre, way of life.

Talking with Chris after the meeting, I complained about some petty business problem. He told me that when he had three years clean, he had some financial problems that almost drove him into bankruptcy.

I remember being shocked that anyone could come close to bankruptcy. The thought was lunacy on my part. I think God saw that and decided I could use a few lessons in how life and business worked, since I thought I was so good at it.

God will send me messages when He wants me to correct my behavior. These can be massively painful or a gentle nudge. Maybe I was meant to receive a message from that conversation with Chris, I don't really know, but I do know I ignored it, even scoffed a bit. I wasn't like him. Financial trouble for me was unthinkable. I was that naïve. I ignored God's nudges, so he sent me a massively painful lesson as I approached Step 6: Become entirely ready to have God remove all of my defects of character.

The first time I worked Step 6 I was two years clean, and my life thus far in recovery had been fairly easy. My business was still riding high, and money was plentiful, as well as time. I had time to go to meetings, hangout with recovery friends, work steps, be with family, and generally clean up in a rather gentle atmosphere. Of course, I took advantage of it. I bought the Ferrari and spent tons more money than I should have.

In 1998 I was riding high. I had borrowed $20,000 to buy into a couple of stocks that turned my stake into $200,000. I took part in a private placement of a small telecom company that turned that $200,000 into $2 million. Life was easy. Work was easy. Once this little company moved out of the speculative stage and began to expand internationally, I began having my clients invest in it also.

Medical doctors, who typically think of themselves as smarter than anyone else, called me leaving voicemails lauding my genius. They paid large fees happily. I was everything my ego told me I could be. My mind's eye could see clearly ahead to vast amounts of personal wealth and national acclaim. I saw myself as another Bob Woodruff (who rode Coca-Cola stock to fabulous wealth). All of the work had been worth it.

But I was so blinded by my own visions of greatness, I couldn't see the warning signs. I didn't want to see them, even as my miracle company's stock price began its tragic nose dive.

One particularly seductive part of the stock market is that on any given day, it can bail you out of almost any problem just by rising or falling in price. So everyday could be the day. When faced with cutting losses, it is never clear whether to sell now and take your loss, or hang on a little longer. Either one of these choices could be a disaster, and you have already committed a great error for buying the stock in the first place. Under pressure, it is very difficult to make a clear call. Throw in the sledgehammer pressure of margin calls, and your brain boils with indecision.

The price of this stock, which peaked in 1998, began a slow, eviscerating decline to $0 in 2001. I had margined all of my personal holdings to the hilt as it rose and was forced to add dwindling cash as it fell.

At this point, I was neither humble, nor thankful for my success. Life was harder than I thought, and I didn't prepare for what God had in store for me next.

When I finally closed my business in 2001, I had destroyed my income and was $800,000 in debt. There was nowhere to turn but to God. I had to put all my affairs at his feet and rebuild. I had to re-start everything on His terms. I had an insufficient salary that would soon disappear, and a family of five who completely depended on me.

The last thing I wanted was to start my career over, humbly going to work for a competitor in their *training* program. That was probably God's point. I had to become willing to do anything, drive a truck, wash cars, run for office, sell door to door. I was forced to leave my personal preferences out of the process and concentrate only on how I could best serve my family, my community, and God. What I wanted no longer counted. I had had my fun. It was time to grow up and get moving. No one else could or would do this for me.

But taking that job meant I could not pay off the credit card companies, and they hounded my family for the first few years. I just could not pay. I was too poor to declare bankruptcy, which would have done nothing because the problem was income. I didn't have any, and my wife and three children had to have money every month.

With the credit card companies, it became war. No one can pay what they do not have, but those venomous collectors didn't care. They began a long campaign of psychic terror, first beating me down, then suing, then winning, then starting all over again.

My income slowly rose to the point where I could just support my family. While that may seem an achievement, I knew better than to congratulate myself. It was God providing for my wife and three children. I was only the vessel. This was very important for me to understand. Even though I may be given assets, it is not intended for me personally. He will let me know when that time comes, but I should not hold my breath. So long as I can be trusted to distribute assets as He wants me to, the process will continue. Oh, and he allows me to live a life far beyond what I deserve. Not a bad deal, really.

I know better than to get too comfortable, or "pat myself on the back" too much. God has given me so many humility lessons that I am afraid of his retribution should I forget that He is the sole source of whatever bounty I receive. That is why I never really know whether it will continue or not. I have to be diligent and examine my motives all the time. I have to stay close to God's Word, and to surround myself with people and activities that bring me clarity. I have to work at it.

After a while, I found there was no reason for me not to be able to improve myself and develop the high-potential God had given me. God wants me to figure this out myself, I know. He had provided me an excellent education, wonderful parents, and a good mind. I am impatient, though, with my progress. Usually it is in prayer that I am reminded how good I have it.

If I don't get discouraged, and just keep pounding away, there is enormous potential for reward down the road (perhaps *way* down the road). Knowing this keeps me going. Every cent is plowed back into the business, the family, and developing relationships, relationships, relationships.

So, am I succeeding? You got me. I *love* God and I am trying to do what He wants, at the pace He wants, to provide for and help those He directs me to. That's all. It is not my business, it is really not my failure or success. It is His will.

* * * * * * *

In Step 6 I had to "become entirely ready to release all of my defects of character". The important words are "entirely" and "all". This is not about doing something part way. That has been an enormous part of the lesson.
If you are like me, you hesitate. That was revealing. Why should I resist removing character defects? It showed me

that reluctance and complacency build up inside us constantly and are in need of constant vetting. After all, I define the defects. They are things that make my life worse. You would think I could discard them without even batting an eye. Curious.

It became plain to me I had a mental block against improving myself. Even though I know something is good for me, I can resist it. Why is there a force within that distracts us with false promises, fanciful thinking and short-sightedness? Without efforts at spiritual maintenance, we are all drifting in the vicinity of a black hole of self-centeredness. We have to act to keep ourselves away. We have to flap our wings to keep from drowning in ourselves.

The good news is this is not new information. People have been fighting these self-destructive human tendencies for thousands of years, so we have some history to go by. That is one of the things that brought the Bible to me in an entirely new light.

We are so small in the scheme of things that our tiny perspectives may become extremely warped and myopic. My tendency was to self-destruct. It began to dawn on me that I really could be doomed. And that doom led to a very healthy desperation. Healthy because it is borne from truth and reality, just like the day I lost all hope in the lockdown unit of the psych hospital. That's when I saw all of my manipulation and brilliant plans crushed under their own weight, with only the cleansing bleach of absolute terror to galvanize my grim realty into a steel foundation of absolute truth. And that realization, for me, was the rock of a new beginning. There was no longer the luxury of illusion, and my ego had been exorcized by the realization that I was up the creek. Humility is clarity. Humility is pure. Submission is the paradoxical power that rises from the ashes, a phoenix of rebirth. With Christ, "all things are made new".

Christ came to save us from our self-centeredness, to help us control ourselves, our natural instincts, and to think ahead using a brain that could conceive self-awareness. He also came to maintain a spiritual condition through ritual, encouragement, and fellowship, so that we may not only live a better life here, but also to plant the seeds for an incomprehensible eternity, and be at ease with the mysteries of the universe.

Chapter Seven

Willingness

One of the most productive changes we can make for ourselves is willingness. It is not action. It is not results. It is the essential preparatory state to do something new, different, awkward, unfamiliar or big. While it is not essential when starting a grand endeavor, it is essential to finish. Like exercise, you may not "feel" willing until after you start. But you must be willing to take action anyway. Often, the feeling of willingness comes after.

Conversely, lack of willingness is deadly for everyone. Yet, very few really understand its power. This becomes dramatically true when the heat is on: to find a job, to support your family, or to stop using.

As a volunteer with my church's Job Networking ministry, I have made myself available to people looking for advice when they are looking for a job. This is one of the most difficult, miserable times a person can experience.

Just when you feel like crawling into a hole with a TV and a box of Oreos, you are expected to go out and put your best foot forward to convince potential employers that you would be wonderful on the job. You have to deal with endless disappointment and discouragement, then pick yourself up and do it all over again. It is horrible. You are talking to people who already have jobs, and are secure, comfortable and confident. How do you sell yourself in these situations? What do you do when you seem to hit a brick wall?

One job seeker called me for advice on his job search. He was in my industry (financial services) focusing on background administration versus marketing and sales, which are the revenue generators. He had fifteen years of experience and was looking unsuccessfully for another "salary plus benefits" position that didn't require client interaction (he didn't like that). As I listened for anything I could correct or offer advice on, that simple lack of willingness raised a red flag.

He was understandably frustrated, but it came across as complaining. He had "tried everything, gone to all of the networking groups," etc., but nothing worked. No one would hire him. Not many would even see him. As his emotions grew, he almost yelled at me, as if I was somehow involved in causing his misery. Not good for him, but it showed me what might be wrong.

Without my prodding, he volunteered that every person he contacted asked him if he could sell, and if he could bring customers with him to their company. He felt offended by this, yet these people were the ones who could solve his financial problems. But he wouldn't stoop to working on commission. It was beneath him.

This is common. Here was a guy, out of work and desperate, yet thinking he was somehow better than others. God was giving him an opportunity to become humble and thus be more powerful, but he refused to step beyond the boundaries of his narrow, past experiences. Well, God may just figure he needed even <u>more</u> misfortune to get his mind right.

This man needed to be willing to do whatever it took, even if the action made no sense to him at the time. Perhaps he needed to loosen his iron clad tunnel vision of what value he could bring to the world. Perhaps he needed to do more, start his own business, or live differently. Perhaps he needed to pray more about what direction God wanted him to take and be willing to do it.

I asked him if he was a Christian, and he said yes. So I explained that in the financial industry, as well as in most industries in today's economy, staff administrative positions are on a death watch. They are an expense item, and are usually only maintained 1) to directly support revenue generating activities, or 2) comply with a regulation. You will never have job security if you cost more than you produce, so the idea of salary is a mirage. My experience is that salary is much less dependable than producing your own revenue. In both cases, you have to perform, but in the latter, you are responsible for other people's assets as well as your own. On a salary you are *taking* money *from* others, so it is adversarial. You are a target. Your absence makes someone else's life better, and that is not a good way to strengthen a relationship. Yet, people do it all the time with their income, one of the most important relationships they have.

As a Christian, I told him, it is helpful to review one's attitude and be willing to submit to a path that may not be familiar or obvious. Submit to God's will. Stop shooting yourself in the foot. In secular terms this would be to submit to Adam Smith's economic "invisible hand" that moves all commerce in a free market system. You are not accommodating the economy, so it has little to offer you. You are expecting the world of business to accommodate you. That is naïve.

"So drop that attitude," I said, "and get humble, and go where you are needed. This is a growing economy in the richest country in the world. You are hurting yourself and need me to tell you so. If anyone else has, you haven't listened."

In fact, I knew of several companies that might actually be able to use someone like him. But until he got his mind right, I could never have confidently recommended him. He would hurt more than he would help.

Another very close friend of mine has been out of a job for a number of months. I've tried counseling him, but he says he wants action. I gave him action but he doesn't do what I say, and then makes himself crazy with worry because things aren't going well. I've tried again and again to make him understand the concept of willingness. Every bit of misery always comes back to that, but he is too young and headstrong to see the enormous obstacles he sets for himself. Although a strong Christian, he is letting pride get in the way. When I see him again, I think I'll use the old trick I was once subjected to in order for him to grasp the concept of surrender.

My very first sponsor sat across from me at a lunch table in the rehab hospital when I had maybe thirty days clean. I was holding the keys to a rental car and he asked for them. Point blank. He had been unsuccessful, thus far, in teaching me about true surrender, and I, like the two cases above, just did not get it.

He looked me in the eye and said, "Give me your car keys." No explanation, no smile, no joke. I was immediately wary. I had only known this guy for a few days, and we were in a psychiatric hospital, with thieves, drug addicts, felons, and all sorts of untrustworthy people. Why did he want my car keys? To prevent me from driving? To steal it? What a weirdo. But, as he stared at me blankly, I reluctantly decided to go along. I gave him the keys. He put them in his pocket. We dropped the subject and continued our lunch. Only hours later, after the concept had a chance to burn into my thick skull, did he return the keys and smile, saying, "Now <u>that</u> is surrender."

Surrender and willingness are part of the humility that helps us obtain real power. Often it is hard to see the end before you do it. You have to learn to follow directions, which is a large part of willingness itself.

One good exercise is to review what we are <u>unwilling</u> to do. We know what we are willing to do, because we do it all the time. However, we may not even realize many of the things that we are unwilling to do. My experience is that these things can paralyze me with problems, unless I regularly examine them thoroughly.

One fellow I know lives in an expensive Northern California town, and is always out of money. In fact, he is fifty years old, smart, able-bodied, but has never been able to adequately support himself. It does not occur to him to move to a more affordable area, or to accept a job that doesn't "feel right". He is childishly unwilling to go where jobs are, or to lower himself to do something that he might not like. Consequently, he ends up living a miserable life of poverty and discomfort because he will not examine his own unwillingness.

The effect on others is usually more widespread than the person in denial realizes, almost by definition. In this case, the man's wife and family are forced to endure the desperation he lacks. It is a terrible thing to see. And it's extremely predictable. Every season brings with it a new excuse for not accepting responsibility. These excuses range from dyslexia to El Nino to oil prices to the mortgage crisis and everything in between.

This guy will not work. Yet millions of hardworking immigrants, right in front of his face, without knowing the language and frequently here illegally, demonstrate the remarkable power of willingness every day.

There is <u>always</u> an excuse available. We lie to ourselves when we grab that excuse, and comfort ourselves by using that as the reason for our failure when the real reason is unwillingness.

This is the heart of addiction. Active addicts will refrain from doing something that will have bountiful benefits for them, because they are unwilling to give up a life that provides them with tragedy, suffering, and death. This is the insanity of addiction.

Throughout recovery, I have repeatedly seen the willingness concept demonstrated and my understanding clarified. It endures the way truth always does. Time and experience clear the window through which I see its wisdom.

Turning over your will and life to God doesn't mean abandoning your responsibilities to yourself or anyone or anything. In fact, it is just the opposite. It imbues in you a responsibility to behave in the way you best understand what He wants you to do. And that could be anything. It may not be what <u>you</u> think is best for you, but it is not the opposite of what you think either. In fact, what we think about ourselves is usually irrelevant. That is a very difficult concept for our egos (particularly mine) to accept. That is why I have to spend a lot of time maintaining my spiritual condition. I still take back my will regularly, and every time it is to unerring misfortune.

Being "willing" is simple, but very hard to do. This is because it goes against the grain of our immediate nature. The good news is that we can change. Like physical exercise, we can re-direct our actions to modify our instincts. The better news is that we can come to enjoy willingness for its own sake, on top of the many, many rewards it brings.

Chapter Eight

Faith

Step 3 in the 12-step program of recovery states, "Make a decision to turn one's life over to the care of a God of your understanding."

The spiritual principle behind this step is faith. It is critical to the development of the recovering addict, and it is a valuable exercise in anyone's spiritual growth. For most of us in recovery, this is the final inward looking step before we start to develop our relationships with others in Steps 4 through 12.

The decision to turn my will and my life over to a higher power was everything that the first two steps, Honesty in Step 1 and Hope in Step 2, had been building toward.

"We are only operating a spiritual kindergarten in which people are enabled to get over drinking and find the grace to go on living to better effect. Each man's theology has to be his own quest, his own affair." This description of recovery was written by Bill Wilson, an early pioneer in 12 step programs. In my own experience, I could not have described it better.

Only after a few years of diligent work to repair my twisted ways of thinking, and most importantly, not using those substances that were spiritual kryptonite to me, was I ready to receive and appreciate the true nature of the higher power that had delivered me from myself and a death sentence. I don't know how God decides to let people in on the truth about all things, but he let me know slowly, step by step, only as I was able to ingest it.

After two years clean, I had three indispensable gifts in my spiritual journey:

1) I knew that I had been delivered from certain death by the grace of a power far greater than myself, although I had no idea what that was.

2) Curiosity—if a power big enough to save me existed, what was it? How did it work? Just the possibilities cast doubt on my long held beliefs. Knowing I could well be wrong about any and all preconceived notions, what is the Truth? What had I missed? What do I need to know?

3) Respect—I have learned by hard experience not to pass judgment on *anyone's* spiritual beliefs. People are nowhere near as stupid, sheltered, or naïve as

my giant ego had previously categorized them. I had to learn to spend less and listen more.

* * * * * * *

My mother died October 12, 2006, and I was there. I am grateful to have been able to share nine clean years with her, truly getting to know her in a new, real way. I had especially been able to understand her deeply religious persona that I had only observed superficially as an outsider before.

Why is faith so powerful? The only thing that has kept me alive, and certainly sane, is faith in God. That faith has only come from hard observation and experience. Many people can receive the message of faith without having to go through what I did. I'm just hard-headed, I guess.

I had to find out about faith myself. For most of my life, it didn't make much sense to me. You certainly don't buy a car "on faith", or put money in a bank "on faith". I looked at faith as a failing. It was something for people to use who were too slow to figure things out on their own.

My discovery was that faith is something we have to fall back on. We <u>are</u> too small, too shallow, and too unwise to figure out reality ourselves. We must have faith to bridge the gap between what is (reality) and what we can comprehend. Our knowledge is so small in the scheme of things that we hardly ever realize how small we are. People a hundred years from now will look back on us with amazement at our ignorance and naïveté. Can we imagine five hundred years ahead? One thousand?

But we must deal with real, difficult issues now. So we are required to act with imperfect information and imperfect perception every day. This is faith. We employ faith all the time, even if our egos are reluctant to admit it.

Faith develops with experience and observation. The more you see and experience two connected events, the more your confidence grows that the pattern will repeat. I have strong faith the sun will rise in the morning, even if I don't know it with certainty.

Importantly, I have found faith to be a fountain of deep, glorious comfort with tools to manage oneself for the better. This has come from a realization that faith, and faith in God, is a special activity with infinite rewards.

Faith allows for commitment, that most powerful human tool. And if it is so powerful, why are we, men in particular, so fearful of it?

Maybe commitment is the "got ya" for men in the same way that pregnancy is the "got ya" for women.

Women's behavior (trust me, anything I know about women's behavior will be a very short section) has been shaped through history by the predatory male, who seeks pleasure but generally receives little consequence from satisfying sexual pleasures. It is the woman who must carry the baby, the woman who carries the consequences by their biological nature of raising the kids. That is why there must be laws to force dads to help with support. These unbalanced consequences make women more cautious in sexual matters.

Men, on the other hand, are more cautious about commitment, particularly in the areas of marriage and finances. Here, women tend to be more predatory. Once consummated by a legal bond, the man tends to be left "holding the bag" of supporting the woman and children financially, as well as facing the more difficult task (than women) of curtailing his natural tendencies and remain monogamous, against his baser instincts. This is good for men, for sure, but historically, the struggle has been a hallmark of male behavior.

As with so many other things, I have found serious commitment to be the exact opposite of what my child-eyes thought it to be. (This concept is starting to have a familiar ring to it, no?) My distrust and unwillingness to take what turned out to be good advice, kept me from exploring and experiencing an entirely new and better world than I would have ever known.

Perhaps the best example of commitment and its benefit is marriage. Sure, having a great wife makes it easier to be grateful, but I didn't always see the gift as well as I see it now.

As a bachelor, my married friends would encourage me to think about settling down. It seemed to me they only wanted others to validate their misery. I couldn't imagine them to be happier than me: living alone, having few friends, or drinking myself silly in bars to the amusement of endless strangers. What a life! I was free to date whoever I wanted. "I just didn't have the ability", as Ron White, popular comedian, jokes. Among other delights of bachelorhood were overturned cars, mornings in strange cities, and incoherent come-ons that were only occasionally successful because of the sheer volume of them! My married friends were actually very worried about me, about my life, and I didn't have the respect to take them seriously. Like they had never been single! No wonder they worried.

I had never intended to be married, much less for a long time. A previous relationship, a live-in arrangement when I was first out of grad school in Philadelphia, ended with her breaking it off because of my drinking. Big deal, I scoffed. I was a single, successful guy. I found a bachelor pad in a high rise on Philadelphia's Benjamin Franklin Parkway. It was an excellent location to finally make myself available to all those lonely, heart-stopping beauties that somehow didn't flock to me quite as well as my charm should have dictated. Probably because I didn't have enough money yet, or wasn't from the area, anything except what it really was. Besides, I thought, I was doing okay.

I wasn't thinking marriage at all when Emily, the younger sister of a childhood friend, came back on the scene. I have no explanation at all for what happened. I had zero control over matters, especially myself. It was so obvious we should be married that I proposed after seeing her for only two weeks. We married after only ten weeks. It was the best thing I have ever done, maybe because I didn't plan or conceive or strategize or force it. It wasn't my idea at all. I just accepted it as reality because there was simply no debate. That is pretty humbling now to think back on it, that the greatest decision in life was done with zero deliberation from me. Think about that. If you cannot conceive of a deliberate and merciful God, you need to be more aware of the world around you.

I discovered that freedom resulted from the commitment of marriage, not confinement. The bond forged between Emily and me is like no other, and it literally saved my life. Many times. Ask anyone who knows us both. Anyone who knows me always enjoys meeting Emily. Many view her as quite a wonder woman and always give her a pat on the back and a telling smile that says they understand the size of the burden she has had to endure!

For me, marriage has been a fountain of wonderful and life-saving discoveries. It has forced me to build the rudiments of character. Fatherhood forced me even further. You just can't do it otherwise. I never would have made the changes required. After all, I hadn't in many, many years of daily opportunity.

The little bit of character forced on me through marriage and fatherhood has made my life easier in a very real, material way. It has allowed me to follow directions.

When I was told to go to lots of meetings, I could, and did. When I was told to not have an opinion for a while, I didn't. I saw that the world did not fall apart without me directing things.

In fact, things improved! This was an extremely embarrassing and humbling thought. It began to dawn on me how much others knew, and how clearly I could benefit from their experience by simply doing what I was told. Doing this allowed me to do far more than I could accomplish myself. The power of not thinking and just following directions not only got me clean, it proved itself in another equally dramatic achievement—running a 26.2 mile marathon.

Marathon training is a God-given example and vivid analogy of the "follow directions" model obtained in recovery. I was told to do what the coach said and I accomplished far more difficult things than I ever thought possible. I ended up running three marathons in 2001 and 2002, and I had never competed in anything before! I am an athlete! And I raised over $11,000 for Leukemia research.

My affinity for drinking water came from training for a marathon. You would be amazed at how good simple ice cold water can taste after running twenty miles on asphalt in the Georgia summer heat!

I drink about two gallons of water a day, not because I am intentionally trying to do something healthy, it's because I keep it around me all the time, and I let my natural reflexes react. I'm getting out of the way of what God wants.

I had gained about fifty pounds in the first year of recovery stuffing my face with anything and everything I could find. I hadn't exercised at all and I felt it. I had tricked my body into thinking and feeling and acting like a 17-year-old, and all of a sudden I landed in this 44- year-old guy's body, way out of shape, overweight, and with zero energy. *I was old.* And I felt every bit of it!

Fortunately as I look back there was a solution, although at the time I wasn't so sure. There was a time when the entire world used to feel better without illegal Class II pain killers, or energy and euphoria inducing amphetamines. Exercise. I was told to hit the gym. I had to accept the dark reality that you can do something that will not only make you feel better, but can make you feel better without having the bag run out of dope, or being arrested for simply trying to up one's comfort level.

The bad news: there was pain involved. In order to feel better in the long term, you had to feel worse in the short term. Damn, *another* paradox!

So I went to the gym. I encountered Audrey, a buxom personal trainer with great, ah..., posture. I'll hire her! At least it will keep me coming back. And it did. I did the right things, though. I didn't hit on her, I invited my wife to meet her, and I behaved myself. Today we are friends, and Audrey still laughs about the wild and bizarre stuff that came out of my mouth during those early workout sessions as I was re-entering our solar system into the land of the living.

After a while, I tried jogging and signed up for a 5k run in my hometown of Roswell. I ran it in forty-eight minutes, a new record for the longest length of time to finish from an actual entrant. I was slow and grunted out cadences to French fries and milkshakes the whole way!

Eventually, I worked myself up to more abuse and began running 10ks. I was really proud to run even four miles, and then I attempted six! I remember telling my father, who was a world class track star (finished eighth in the country in the Olympic trials for the decathlon in 1948), avid tennis player, and the elegant natural that I never was. He was proud of me and it felt good.

I could never go very fast in 10ks, and it would have been discouraging had I not been in recovery and constantly reminded that I was lucky to be alive, lucky to even be walking, much less jogging, much less competing! So I started to get into it. I subscribed to running magazines, and tried to keep myself encouraged.

I saw a magazine ad for an Atlanta area group called Team-in-Training, sponsored by the Leukemia Society, that organized practice runs on Saturdays for anyone who wanted to practice. Why not? Maybe I could pick up some tips about how to run these 10ks a little faster, or at least learn how to make them less miserable.

So I went one Saturday, fearful that it would be some sort of Parris Island torture session, but it was just the opposite. Everybody made it easy. A group of us started on a four mile run. Many people stopped when they felt like it, slowed when they felt like it, and the group stretched out to accommodate whatever the individuals wanted to do. I could handle this!

Everyone was pleasant, in a very cool sort of way. The guy running beside me was about my age and he remarked that he'd had two heart attacks. Wow, I thought. Then he said he'd also run a marathon, and was training now for another in about six months. In Bermuda. What? He was just jogging along with me. A marathon? That's the Mt. Everest of all athletics. How in the world? Then it came from his lips. "You could too." What was that again?

To me, and to most people, the idea of running 26.2 miles in competition is unimaginable. Three miles can be unimaginable. But twenty-six miles is so far outside my realm of possibility, it didn't even register. It was like another language. I and the word "marathon" had never been seen in the same state, much less had some sort of relationship.

That's why the thought of a 13.1 mile half-marathon was as far from my world as the 26.2 full marathon. Once you get beyond six or seven, it's all squarely in the set of activities only seen on TV done by oddly motivated fanatics from whatever world they were living in.

But Bermuda? Hey, I heard that was a heckuva place. These organizers sure think "location" like I do.

How about pain? Hey, I have dedicated my life to the avoidance of pain and maximization of my personal comfort. That notion is a cancer cell to be attacked by my natural comfort-seeking hemoglobins.

When I run three miles, I am dying. *Dying.* Running the fourth, fifth, and sixth are beyond hell for me. But these marathoners ran the equivalent of four 10ks in a row, with no break! This was a severe test for a fit athlete; it was insanity to consider it for me.

"Yes, if you can run the four miles we have almost finished today, you can run a marathon," said my congenial running mate that summer Saturday morning in Buckhead. Little did he know my brain was screaming "REJECT THIS THOUGHT, REJECT THIS THOUGHT."

"We show you how," he said. "You just follow directions. I did four and I've had two heart attacks, and I am the same age as you, Lee."

DOES NOT COMPUTE. DOES NOT COMPUTE. INPUT INCOMPATIBLE. INPUT INFECTING PROTOCOL. REJECT. RATIONALIZATION SECTORS TO FULL MOBILIZATION.

By the time we returned from the introductory jog, I had decided *not* to think about running a marathon. I signed up to start training. Ahhh, the power of not thinking.

That action was fortuitous. For the first time since the example of recovery, I found another stark example of how, by turning off your own judgmental self, you can do far more than you ever envisioned. When always assessing how am I doing, and not actually doing, I waste enormous amounts of energy. If I stopped to wonder if I could do it, I would not have carried on. There was no way I could conceive of me doing it, so such thoughts were useless at best, fatal at worst.

The wonderful volunteer organizers of Team in Training, led by Dr. Tommy Owens in Atlanta, were very experienced in transforming skeptical newcomers into doing something completely beyond their perceived ability, including raising enormous amounts of money for a life-saving cause.

The uncanny similarities to recovery illustrated a new life-long model for doing incredibly difficult things. And by incredible I mean stuff that you, deep down, feel there is no friggin' way you can do. Since we normally don't try things we're convinced we can't do, these abilities don't usually come up unless we are supremely motivated, as in life-threatening situations. If you can't quit smoking, there is nothing like a little cardiac arrest to make you more open to suggestions.

Getting clean and sober is one of those things I had to do, but didn't think I could. In fact, I had to get to that point in order to do it. Bizarre. Explain that to someone coming in off the street with most of their brain soaked in chemicals. It's difficult.

Here are elements from both recovery and marathon training that got me across the 26.2 mile finish line:

1. Be willing to follow directions.
2. Turn your brain off. Do what you are told to do that day.
3. Never judge these directions; just do them.
4. Trust your coach/sponsor/instructor. Don't trust yourself. Turn everything over to them.
5. Keep your expectations low.

The first thing the Team in Training people do is make it fun. After that, they completely lower your expectations that training will be anything but misery. However, they told me the way to accomplish this unthinkable task was not obvious to most of us. So we had to trust them. They had been doing this at least ten years and trained thousands of marathon neophytes. They had developed a six month program of physical training and fund-raising that worked, and it was not obvious to any of us.

A schedule for each day leading up to the marathon had been constructed and distributed. Every week there were group runs, which I thought would be doubly miserable, since they no doubt would require me to keep up with my Olympic cohorts. Oops, there I went—thinking again.

The first thing I noticed about the training schedule was not the running days. I was already expecting an anguishing number of those. I was surprised to see how much rest was commanded by the schedule. There was almost as much rest scheduled as training. Incredible. Now that is something I can do. Also, not only could we eat whatever we wanted, we should eat a lot. I can do that pretty well, too.

The group training sessions were very well organized by cheerful volunteers who provided water stops, fresh bagels at the end, and even masseuses! They really knew what they were doing. Importantly, they treated us with dignity. We were made to understand that we were the life-blood of cancer research. And almost all of them were there because Leukemia had tragically devastated them personally. We were treated with honor. We were treated like they understood the awkward discouragement a newcomer must overcome, and they were pulling for us, proud for every day that we seemed to understand the deeper, serious purpose of our task, and helped carry their cross with our sweat and our commitment to something we still had yet to fully grasp. We were treated like a newcomer to the rooms of recovery, the most important person at the meeting.

My oldest son, John, was nine when I started recovery. He is now nineteen, and a fine, accomplished athlete and scholar at Florida State University. When he was seventeen, he was on his high school's varsity football team. He lettered in football, wrestling, and track as a junior, and was on the state championship football squad his senior year.

His accomplishments were light-years beyond anything I did athletically. I was so impressed, I asked him simply, "How did you mature so well over your teen years?"

"You don't realize it's happening (growth) until you look back," he said.

"But how did you develop the patience and discipline so young?" I probed.

"Football is really just a bunch of guys fooling around, having fun basically," he answered. "Team sports just taught me a lot about other people, working, and doing things with them."

My first two years clean were much like a high school student growing up. I learned some very basic skills to keep myself alive. I learned a little about spirituality, but God didn't think I was ready to advance too much, or even attend church, until I had a solid spiritual foundation. That foundation can be boiled down into two essential traits: curiosity and respect.

Before I got clean Emily wanted our family to belong to a church, for her own sanity at least. She knew that religion should be a part of our children's lives, as it had been a part of her and my young life. Like my mother, she was raised in the small Georgia town of Americus where, like most small southern towns, the churches were often the social hub of the community. Everyone generally attended. Church was a natural part of her upbringing. God has consistently had a strong and enduring presence in her life. She tells me now that she prayed often for me and our family during the dark times. She may have told me this then but I dismissed it as weakness or some lack of appropriate courage on her part. It makes me shudder to think what this wonderful woman went through.

When we did go to Church, I made the experience miserable. Well into my 40's, I still looked at Church as a 13-year-old, since I had carried this intellectual rejection of Church as everyman's self-made myth since my early teens. Worst of all, I knew it. My ego had come up with a very interesting reason why such a conclusion, by a 13 year-old with little or no study in that area, could deduce that religion was a sham invented by weak-minded people who could not handle the Truth. And the reason was that I was simply brilliant. Yes, I was a genius. My superior intellect was above religion. I could handle the Truth that religion was just mythology. Its purpose was to control the masses. It sought to prevent the open-minded exploration of Truth, which is always best done without any preconceived notions.

After all, didn't religion cause most of the suffering in history by fueling the reasons to make war? Wouldn't God, if there was one, use his Almighty power to save suffering and innocent children who die by the hundreds every hour? And if there was no God, wouldn't man probably *invent* one? Surely he would have to, for the mass of lower level intellect couldn't handle the Truth like I and the "Intelligentsia" (as one fellow snob at Ivy League Penn put it) could handle it?

This concept of religion not only held force with me for more than thirty years, it was steeled and forged by an incredible university education.

Undergraduate study at FSU, a large state university, accelerated this intellectual snobbery, and the indulgent hedonism it allowed, with glee. But going to the Ivy League, the University of Pennsylvania in 1978 for graduate school, put a Trident missile boost to my self-centered, Godless take on the world.

What was interesting at this point was that I started drinking very heavily at Penn. For such an intellectual snob, I found myself cast in with people far, far ahead of me in cranial capacity and storehouses of knowledge. I was alone. I knew no one. I was in a doctoral program in the most prestigious business school in the world, and I had not even received my Masters degree yet. My first class at Wharton was in economics, and the professor didn't even speak! He went to the board and began writing incomprehensible calculus equations, one after the other, without comment for an hour.

Toward the end of the hour, after the prof had filled about four blackboards with this derivation and proof of fifty steps and I was still trying to figure out how he got from step one to step two, a snobby, short French student asked him, "Is this an open or closed economy?" I remember that after almost thirty years because it told me at the time that he, a heavily accented *foreigner*, was actually keeping up with this mad professor! *Everyone* kept up, but me.

To my left in the class was an amiable but extreme geek from Hong Kong, who I later learned had already written a college text book on Statistics. He was my classmate! Another classmate had not only been an undergrad at Harvard, he already had a Masters from Harvard in Math. All of these "whiz kids" were really depressing.

I was a small fish in an ocean of sharks, but I could contend with the best of them in two areas: drinking and drugs. Now that, I could do. My ego latched on to that like a leech as my self-esteem plummeted. As I would later learn, much later unfortunately, this was a typical alcoholic combination, an outsized ego with shrinking self-esteem. These are the building blocks of denial. As we say in the rooms of recovery, we are egomaniacs with inferiority complexes.

So much for intellectual growth.

As the increasing alcohol and drugs fueled my ego-charged decay, my slippery slope steepened. My decline picked up a pace. I didn't need God. I didn't need anybody. Denial, fantasy, and arrogance increasingly replaced humility and love.

Faith had been pushed aside -- unappreciated, unnecessary, and very uncool. Over the next twenty years, this would come back to haunt me deeply. My disregard for faith almost killed me. In doing so, however, it ended up saving me forever.

Faith allows us to do that. Faith in God, one God, the God of the Bible, gets us even further. Go through Proverbs a few times and tell me that most of these thousand-year-old concepts aren't true today. And most are not intuitively obvious to our self-seeking, carnal nature. The Proverbs, and the Bible in general, was given to us to save us from ourselves.

Faith in Christ, in my experience, has simply been an enormous jump to the next level of understanding of what we are dealing with here. And wow, what a step! But I had to understand the whole concept of God before I could begin to grasp the enormity and the reality of Christ and the Trinity.

Chapter Nine

Miracles

It is a miracle I am alive at all. It is also a miracle that groups of recovering addicts and alcoholics can gather in one room, at an appointed hour, for years on end, to self-sustain the spiritual growth that keeps them alive. Against all odds. It's not science; it's a miracle.

Science is concerned with things that are measurable beyond any subjective judgment. A Jewish American scientist must view a rock (or a lizard, or a star, or a microbe) in the same way an atheist Chinese scientist, or a Christian Swedish scientist sees that rock, so they can share and utilize their common discoveries. And there is no shortage of things left for discovery.

But "discovered science" is but a micro subset of all knowledge. When pondering the "non-scientifically verified yet" knowledge, it helps me to separate it into two parts.

The first part is what we encounter and must deal with but don't know enough about to fully explain scientifically. This might be gravity, love, universe origins, life, etc.

The second part is what we do not encounter at all, and therefore don't know what we don't know.

Historically, there has always been great danger in underestimating the enormity of these last two. It is tempting, and technically true, to think we could possibly know everything about all things, but we have yet to discover even a hint of how much we do not know.

The telling thing for me is that the higher up you go in the scientific community, or in any serious pursuit of Truth, the more we discover how little we know. I often find that the greatest possessors of experience and knowledge are humbled by the enormity of our ignorance. And no shortage of God believers among them.

Possibly, we may eventually have scientific knowledge of everything. As a Christian, that would mean heaven, God, how that alpha/omega thing works, and the secret to Dick Clark's youth. But, I submit, it will be a long, long time before that happens.

Most people agree that we must constantly trust things we cannot control. We have to trust that our car will start, that the other guy won't change lanes into ours, that we can earn a living, that the banks will honor our checks, etc. As we repeat these acts over and over, our trust builds.

Soon we don't have to think about it any more. We know it will happen.

We <u>need</u> to trust others, even though they, like us, are unreliable and untrustworthy to various degrees. We cannot <u>know</u> they will do something in the same way that we <u>know</u> gasoline plus oxygen plus a match will equal flame (scientific knowledge), but we can predict intelligently without scientific knowledge. We have to, because most of life is uncertain. Familiarity gives the knowledge.

Why then should it be difficult to trust in something that is perfect? Perfectly reliable, perfectly predictable. For me, one reason was my inability to see the evidence right before my eyes. Another was my inability to grasp something as enormous as God with my limited brain and imagination. Both of these are human failings, problems within our own minds, not God's. These are failings that people will probably look back on from a thousand years in the future and wonder why we were so blind, just as we look back one thousand years and see how limited our scope was then. We must realize how tiny our current concepts must be in the grand march of all time and all things.

Yet, our egos tell us we know a lot. They comfort us into believing we should be able to understand everything. This arrogance blinds us to serious tools we desperately need, and need to have faith in, to save ourselves from ourselves.

I am excited about science, what it does, and what it will discover about us. I fully expect science will someday explain all of the mysteries of life and spirit. But until that time, we have faith to fill in the gap. This gives us the power of commitment and trust to not only live, but to live abundantly.

We are not going to believe anything just because we are told it is true. For many years I was frustrated by the seemingly cyclical reasoning that God was true only because the "Bible says so". To a fellow believer, who already believes Biblical authority, this is sufficient. To the non-believer, it makes no sense it all. I dismissed the notion of miracles with equal ease.

As a non-believer, I made the mistake of thinking that this was what all Christians relied on to convert from non-belief to belief. I over-simplified what I thought was a logical flaw in the thinking of millions.

Eventually, I found out that I was wrong about the vast majority of adult Christians. They did not believe because the "Bible said so," rationalizing in some way this blatant begging of the question. They believed because of increasing evidence and truth that they discovered for themselves.

This gave me great pause about everything I thought I knew about adult Christians. These were bright, hard-working, successful people, who had to deal with reality all of their lives, and didn't have the luxury of pinning their futures, and their families, on a pleasant fantasy. These people were real. Real problems. Real grief. Real doubts. Real responsibilities where they couldn't afford to be wrong. Kind of like me.

There was something at work here I had never respected. This pause, this withholding of judgment, was seminal in opening my closed mind that had been sealed shut by intellectual arrogance and assumptions made without evidence. These people do deal with life. I glanced at the Church's prayer list and saw a long, long string of tragic circumstances these people published among them, and faced as a congregation. This was not the act of denial or naiveté, of which I had become an expert. This was courage and truth.

I breathed in a jet stream of new found respect for these fellow travelers. I was humbled by my own flawed and childish thinking. I was curious.

So the three great pistons for ongoing character growth were given to me: respect, humility, and curiosity.

Thusly prepared, my discoveries opened into a new world of possibility beyond the vast horizon of my own very robust imagination. That strengthened my ability to see what was being revealed. That, rooted in an emerging spiritual awakening, was a true miracle.

Isn't it interesting that we are among miracles all the time, but don't recognize them as such? If this seems like a strange sentence, you are exactly like I was for a very long time.

To a 13-year-old smart aleck, a clever, rebellious college student, and an ambitious corporate capitalist, people of faith seemed so simple, so easy to explain.

They seemed to keep their lives straight-forward. They did what their parents taught them to do. They kept things predictable, and stayed within their own, tiny, comfort zone. You can see this by just looking at them gathering for Sunday services at Church, all clean and pressed, their kids all bubbly and bright, their fake smiles beaming at each other. Ugh...

In active addiction, I would watch them from a blood shot gaze. Rolling by in my out-all-night Mercedes, trying to creep back to the house after dawn, hoping the cops wouldn't stop me, hoping my wife wouldn't care. I watched with disdain as I made my way back after a three day binge. Me, the party animal. If they only knew how great it was to be me. I was insane.

I didn't understand much about God until I was ready to understand it for myself. I was required to ponder the concept of an entity that was God, and that God was the God of the Bible and the Jews. That alone is a lot for this small mind of mine to wrap around, so I needed a few years before advancing to the next step.

Isn't it weird that even the most cynical and atheist among us (again, I was there a long time myself) can live with stuff, to know things a lot weirder than an "unseen" God, which of course is pretty weird in itself?

For example, no one knows how gravity works, but we certainly have faith in it every day. We cannot explain it, but for practical reasons we have to accept it. If gravity were something that only existed in the next neighborhood, and we never had to deal with it, I'll bet the whole notion of it would be treated by many as the spiritual notion of what God is today.

We cannot explain life itself. Ask any scientist. We do not know that our universe is all there is, in fact you can probably bet it isn't. Just because we don't have to deal with the immeasurable parts of the cosmos doesn't mean they don't exist.

Why was it so difficult for me to accept for so long that most of the undiscovered parts of reality were unimaginable to me, and my brain, and my world, an area a heck of a lot smaller than I think, and certainly would like to think?

The notion of God is well within man's imagination, many peoples' imagination. I just had to accept that I cannot, and will not, understand it all. In fact, the further you get in any field, you'll notice an increase in the admission of the true experts that they actually know very little, even though they have come to know a great deal more than any other living human. Newton and Einstein admitted this. Part of awareness is living with the reality of how much we really don't know, not how much our arrogance tells us we do.

The greatest miracle to me is that there seems to be a stable, reliable and workable process for hopelessly addicted, self-destructive, and insane human rubbish to not only become and stay clean, but to have access to an unusual wisdom that reveals the spiritual power of God. In everything. I see this day after day, meeting after meeting.

The other is the awareness that all of God's creation envelops us every day, in our children, in nature, in these neat little tools we have invented for ourselves (stoves, cars, gas stations, laptops, etc.). Think about it.

Consider the power of prayer. Many think this is silly. And who really blames them? It sure seems silly on the surface. But I am convinced those that do not appreciate the power of prayer have not done it enough.

During my active addiction, my wife prayed for me a lot, along with others. There was no reason to think I could successfully recover. *None.* In fact, if you asked most people at the time, I was more likely to die than to live. That's what they said then, and I now agree with that grim assessment. The sad fact is that most people who have crossed that line from heavy use into addiction do not recover. Something like eighty percent fail.

You cannot tell me my recovery is not a miracle. *I should be dead.* At best, I should be in prison, with all hope for a productive life as a family man and productive citizen demolished. My beautiful family, charming children, and my kind wife, who brought nothing on themselves, would have been strewn among the destruction of their father's demise. Their childhood was shaping up to be a long tragedy of hope slipping away amid embarrassment, humiliation, and pain.

But it was not to be. My children did not have to grow up with a sociopath. They don't have to spend their adult lives with such scars. Many people in recovery went through a childhood hell that my children were spared.

Without a doubt, this is the one gift, among many mind you, that I can remember when I forget how blessed I am. Whenever I am angry, I try to remember my blessings. You can't be angry and grateful at the same time.

They say that injustice is not getting what you deserve, and that justice is getting what you deserve. But Grace - GRACE - is getting what you do NOT deserve. I have received far more than I ever deserved or imagined. By the GRACE of GOD go I.

I am alive and free and I don't deserve it. Unfortunately, I forget this frequently, and have to be reminded. So be it. This is the purpose of spiritual maintenance. Through the Bible, the books of recovery, and the many, many messages that come to me from others, I am able to relax in the serene luxury of His Grace, in the deep awareness that all of this is real.

Things that would be considered miracles today will be easily explained a few centuries ahead. By going back in time, we can see the brevity of an era in time. Once, the thought of flight was considered impossible, as was the concept of a round earth. Ironically, using gods to explain all perplexing natural phenomenon was as naïve then as saying that only science today has an exclusive on knowledge.

Much that is known and used today is unexplainable by science. Why is it so difficult to recognize the self-imposed, and critically necessary, conservatism of science? Why is it that advanced scientists find themselves encountered by greater realms of questions as they accumulate known facts. Many scientists are drawn to the spiritual out of respect for their own observations. There is no incompatibility with faith and science. Faith is just knowledge science has yet to prove, which is almost everything.

To me gravity, magnetism, the atom, the spark of life at conception, the earth's delicate life-supporting ability, the Bible's interwoven fabric of wisdom, a heavy jet rising off the runway, a child's discovery, the love of a mother, and grace of God are all miracles. And they are all real.

Chapter Ten

Relationships

As a kid, I was gregarious and had lots of fun friends. Addiction and denial completely suffocated this, replacing it with ever increasing isolation and estrangement, which is exactly what I hear thousands of others say when describing this disease.

I slowly came to realize that everything: every check, every kiss, every compliment, every business transaction, and every favor I would need to avoid both prison and renewed active addiction, everything I ever received would come to me by the hand of someone else.

What I had to learn was the achingly simple lesson that I should be more respectful and willing to have positive relationships with others, which is best accomplished by helping them over their problems and pain.

This was the beginning of a whole new way of approaching relationships. In fact, it's a way of getting not only what you want, but more than you want. It wasn't obvious to me that you do yourself a great service by serving others. It has taken me a long time to comprehend that, even though I have been told it all my life.

I came to realize that all my relationships were actually one relationship with God, who fed Himself through these many, many channels. If I had taken enough time in prayer and meditation, and if I kept my eyes and mind open to what was going on around me, I would have understood this.

In the end, relationships, the things I'd been destroying for years and years, and the commitments that are built to bind them, are gifts for our own salvation from God. If you want to quit struggling so hard to have people do business with you, forget yourself for a while. Don't worry, we are so naturally self-centered you will never neglect yourself. The best we can hope for is temporary relief from our selfish ways. Like drugs, many things seduce us with apparent plenty. The reward is often the opposite: deterioration, rejection, and failure. To grow up is to see beyond the immediate.

To a child (or a childish adult), the commitments that bind these relationships seem, on the outside, to be oppressive. Fear and immaturity mask the spiritual and real rewards that come from the growth and maturity needed to make a commitment; in particular, marriage. What was first thought as restrictive (especially from a licentious, self-centered, ego maniac), was shown to me to be the opposite: freeing, exhilarating, and actually saving me from myself. Maybe I am lucky to have a very good spouse, but I deserved to have lost her and my children long ago. There are so many benefits to commitments, and I try to make them. I pray to God to help me. He does, but not always in an easy way. If, idiotically, I over commit to things I can't do or that serve no purpose, I have to make amends, apologize, fix it, and come face to face with the reality of how far I have to go.

Commitments are good. Children seem to react well to them. Other people have been committed to me in ways and to degrees I never realized until I needed them. And boy, have I needed them. The commitment of others has saved my life over and over. So the idea of being "saved" is not completely strange to me.

Many people in life already know a lot about these discoveries. Many call it growing up. Many people did not have to go through the pain I did to learn the lessons. And to them I take my hat off.

In fact, many people have banded together to form organizations to help them help each other. One of those I encountered early on was Freemasonry, which you have to enter on faith, of which I knew little. Once in, I was afforded a glimpse into the private lives, problems, and secrets of other guys trying to make their way through the often difficult realities of life. I listened and learned a lot. It was the same anonymous groups that had started me in recovery. These people, by revealing themselves honestly, gave me great insight into far more universal spiritual lessons.

Growing in Freemasonry was remarkably synergistic to an active recovery. But I dare not replace recovery with the Lodge. I had to remember my situation. When time constraints forced me to lighten up on one of my commitments, it became clear to me, with the absolute love and support of my brother Masons, that my Lodge presence would be the accommodating activity. I will always be a Master Mason, a member in good standing with Roswell Lodge #165. For all they have given me, I look forward to the day that I can repay this wonderful, and much misunderstood, fellowship.

But the far greatest organization, whose concepts and principles kept taking on a more and more familiar light as my mind opened and the slow dawning of awareness in reality took hold, was the Church.

When I first walked into the "Crosstalk" adult Sunday School class, I didn't know anyone. I wandered around in the halls after everyone had gone to their customary class, but I wasn't alone. I had prayed for God to guide me. I hadn't wanted anything from this request and didn't want action. I only wanted to be aimless, to give my brain a little rest. I thought it was okay here in Church. Other places I might have thought were a "cop-out", some form of laziness over which to fret, but not here. That was a big reward for not being in charge.

There were thirty or thirty-five people in the class, well dressed, about fifty 65-year-olds, men and women, politely seated in front of a small lectern. They all looked up as I walked in and sat as inconspicuously as possible in the first seat by the door. The class had already started so there was no small talk. The speaker had just been introduced and was walking up to the front.

Everyone settled back looking ahead to the class leader's position. As he strode to the front to teach the class, I noticed a small, dark blue book in his hand. In this setting one expected that to be a Bible, but to me it looked like the paperback version of recovery's "Big Book". What an imagination I had. I didn't think anything more of it until he cleared his throat. From the front, he looked sheepishly at his long–time friends, classmates, and this new stranger who had just walked in.

"I am Joe, and I am an alcoholic," he said in a deep voice. You could have heard a pin drop. Mouths dropped open, especially mine. I couldn't believe what I just heard.

Little did I know that Joe was a recovering alcoholic with four years sober, about one more than me. He had been a member of this "Crosstalk" Sunday School class for many years. No one knew that he was in recovery or that this was his "coming out." He had volunteered to lead the class in a Bible Study, but decided to show his fellow members what a recovery meeting was like by conducting the class as one.

His nervousness showed. He had no idea how the class would react to this deeply personal confession. It takes courage to do that, largely because our mind makes us dread this sort of admission to others, maybe because we have zero control over the reaction of others, and that discomforts us. Most of the time, such fears are far overblown.

I learned later that both Joe and the members of the class had been concerned that I, as a guest no one knew, would be put off by the emphasis on alcohol recovery in the class and might not return. It was so ironic that this was the most comforting topic anyone could have picked for a recovering alcoholic like me!

About twenty minutes into the class, things began to bog down for Joe. Recovery meetings are meant for discussion by any number of participants. It is usually spontaneous and lively, not well adaptable to the lecture format of a Sunday School class. As it began to drag, and I knew Joe could use some help, I decided that even as a complete stranger, I would help my newest brother in recovery.

"Hello," I said. "I am Lee, and I am an alcoholic." Everyone turned to look at me in bewilderment, especially Joe! I shared my experience and explained why I spoke up, and how I came to sit in this class. It was one of the clearest examples of God's work in my and Joe's life. Of course, I knew I was in the right place. I stayed and became an active member of that class because I knew for certain this was where He wanted me to be. For months afterwards, everyone thought Joe had planted me just for show in his presentation. All were astounded to learn that I actually was a stranger, led solely by a respect and curiosity and willingness brought about by God.

Through my action of being willing to make amends to God, I was given immediate, visible, and great reward, far beyond what I could have comprehended. Through my activity in that class, more accurately through the relationships I developed with those people, I was brought into a clearer understanding of who this higher power truly was. I was given patient and scholarly teachers to not only show me how to exercise and to feel great physically, but to appreciate the enormity of God, and the benefits of studying His word.

When I had a gut-wrenching reversal in business, I found that members of that class had a wealth of experience, strength, and solutions. They had been places I had never been and learned to live life with increasing humility in God's will. It worked for a lot of people. They were not mindless faces showing up at Church because their Momma made them, but real people having to face life on life's terms, and not only surviving, but prospering. They gave it all, freely, to me.

When I began to admit to God, to myself, and to other human beings the exact nature of my past wrongs, my whole approach to relationship forming changed. It became a positive, truthful relationship which blossomed in the sun of reality. The more I focused on serving those I met, with respect and humility, the more they became interested in me. The more I looked into what made other people tick, the more I realized how much I tended to judge "books by their covers", and missed so much of the good in others. As I realized how out of whack my intuition could be, I found myself finding deep, valuable relationships that last and, grow, and give my life a meaning beyond what I have ever known.

This is especially true with God, Christ, and the Holy Spirit. Clearing the wreckage of my past years' spiritual disdain through humility, respect, and genuine curiosity, has paved the way for all other relationships to blossom and has benefited myself and others exponentially. This, to me, is Grace.

Chapter Eleven

Humility

Most of my spiritual growth comes unexpectedly. While usually forced on me through pain, I view this growth as ignorance transitioning into clarity. That takes a willing and humble mindset.

If I could learn things that I already understood, I would not gain much! When you think about it, isn't almost everything that is new to us strange, or not make sense to us at first? Did we initially understand how college would lead to a better life? Or that putting a letter in a box on the corner would make it end up at your friend's house in another state? Or that submission to God gave us power?

For me, misfortune had to be heaped on me to create the humility to learn what I needed to learn, and do what I needed to do. Whether your family cannot eat until you find a job, your child is diagnosed with leukemia, or everything you depend on betrays you, our egos still wrestle for survival. Our egos cause us to cling to things and behavior we believe we need. Sometimes we think we're entitled, sometimes we think we are essential. Only in desperation are these character defects burned away. Only in brokenness do we see our true insignificance. Only in hopelessness do we begin to emerge from the darkness of our conceit. In humility, we are lifted from our prisons. We are liberated by truth and we are flushed with gratitude and made calm. We find ourselves gaining strength in a way we never knew. We have survived. In gratitude we have found a way to live with whatever reality is set before us.

Throughout recovery, I had this concept demonstrated and my understanding of it clarified. It endures the way Truth endures. Time and experience clear the window through which I see this, like Windex to glass.

It was especially made clear in recovery Steps 4 through 7. After I had taken a thorough personal inventory of all the things I had done to others, and admitted it to another human being (Step 5), the next process was to become "entirely ready to have God remove all of these defects of character." This was, and is, a lot harder than it looks. The rewards, as usual, are commensurately larger. The first time I worked Step 6 I had two years clean, and my life thus far in recovery had been fairly easy (that would change in short order!). My business was still riding high and money was plentiful, as well as time.

Most addicts come into recovery without any money and are desperate to find work when they are often unemployable. They must pay the bills and work out the enormous financial mess in which they usually find themselves.

Not me. For some reason God gave me a two year grace period from financial worries, so I had plenty of time to go to meetings, hangout with recovery friends, work steps, be with family, and generally clean up in a rather gentle atmosphere. Of course, I took advantage of it. I bought the Ferrari and spent tons more money than I should have. And He intended to let me have it with financial hardship a little later on, when I guess He figured I could handle it and needed it.

In Step 6 we want to become entirely ready to have all of our character defects removed. The important words are "entirely" and "all". This is not about doing something part way, and it's been an enormous part of the lesson.

If you are like me, you hesitate. That was revealing. Why should I resist removing character defects? It showed me that reluctance and complacency build up inside us constantly, and therefore need constant vetting. After all, I define the defects. They are things that make my life worse, and you would think I could discard them without even batting an eye. Curious.

So it became plain to me that there was a mental block against improving myself. Even though I know something is good for me, I can resist it. Why is there a force within that distracts us with false promises, fanciful thinking, and short-sightedness? Without efforts at spiritual maintenance, we are all drifting into the vicinity of a black hole of self-centeredness. We have to act to keep ourselves aware. We have to flap our wings to keep from drowning in ourselves.

The good news is, this is not new information. People have been fighting these self-destructive human tendencies for thousands of years, so we do have some history to go by. That is one of the things that brought the Bible to me in an entirely new light.

Christ came to save us from our self-centeredness, to control ourselves and our natural instincts, and to think ahead using a brain that can conceive self-awareness. To maintain a spiritual condition through ritual, encouragement, and fellowship, so that we may not only live a better life here, but to plant the seeds for an incomprehensible eternity and be at ease with the mysteries of the universe.

This is very humbling, at least to me. We are very small in the scheme of things, our tiny perspectives extremely warped and myopic, and our tendency is to self-destruct. It began to dawn on me that we really are doomed. And that doom led to a very healthy desperation. Healthy because it is borne from truth and reality, just like the day I lost all hope in the lockdown unit of the psych hospital. All of my brilliant manipulations had been crushed under their own weight. Only the cleansing bleach of absolute terror could galvanize my acceptance of the grim truth. Only through this process could a forge a solid enough foundation to shoulder the work ahead. I was humbled, broken insect. But I was standing on the rock of a new beginning. No longer could I afford illusion. My ego had been exorcized by the realization that I was up the creek. Humility is clarity. Humility is pure. Submission is the paradoxical power rising from the ashes, a phoenix of rebirth, and with Christ, "all things are made new."

Step Seven of most twelve step programs reads: "Humbly ask Him to remove my shortcomings." This follows Step Six, which prepares us to be "entirely ready to have God remove all of his defects of character."

Turning over your will and life to God does not mean abandoning your responsibilities to yourself, or anyone, or anything. In fact, it is just the opposite. It imbues in you a responsibility to behave in the way you best understand what He wants you to do. And that could be anything. It certainly is not what you think is the best for you, but it is not the opposite of what you think either. In fact, I'm sorry to say, what we think about ourselves is irrelevant. That is a very difficult concept for our egos, particularly mine, to accept. That is why I have to spend a lot of time maintaining my spiritual condition. I take back my will regularly, and every time it is to unerring misfortune.

A word on attitude. Tragically, it is easy for us to

lose the attitudes that saved us. We have to keep seeking them out. Humility and gratitude paved the way for us to recruit God's power in our personal problems.

I once had a consulting assignment at a client's business, where the top problem was an employee who did not yet know how to apply spiritual principles in the work place. He was a long-time recovering addict and was diligent in his recovery program, something that had certainly inspired me to a higher standard in my own recovery. I have known him for a long time.

He was extremely intelligent and was an excellent worker, except that he was hard to work with among the employees, and most importantly with the owner, whom he felt entitled to deride and lampoon in front of other employees. The owner had simply had enough, and this man, married with a pregnant wife, was scheduled to be fired.

That was the situation when I arrived. My assignment, after solving this employee problem, employee, was to make and help implement a strategic plan for this company. They were on the verge of exploding with prosperity. My plan had to include whatever re-tooling was necessary to prepare all departments into one efficient, large capacity, growth machine.

It was exciting, and I knew I had very little time, and even smaller patience from the owner, to deal with this man and his problems.

His ego had become so inflated he considered almost all of the other employees buffoons or idiots. He referred to himself twice as a Ferrari trying to work among Hyundais.

That was a red flag. Anyone that openly thinks very highly of himself is usually wrong. This man had lost his humility and his respect for others, and it was killing him. The owner and he did not talk, and this lack of communication fanned the flames of his fantasy. He thought himself indispensable. He was actually about to get fired.

And he did. It was a brutal lesson for him, one he might have avoided if he'd only bent to God's will, rather than resisted it. If he had been more open to his own fallibility, he might have been able to adjust in a less jarring way.

In all of these cases, and for anyone facing a difficult task, I suggest some version of the following "To Do" list, which implements the power of humility and willingness.

A. Attitude

　　1. Become willing to take directions from a trusted source.

　　2. Resolve to do all of the following tasks completely.

　　3. When you fail at any one task, start over.

　　4. Understand that to "take direction" means

to not question the order. You have no opinion and you are not to judge or second guess anything. You just do it, especially the parts that do not make sense or those you do not want to do.

5. Toss your personal preferences out the window.

6. Give up any notion that you know what God wants you to do or be.

7. In my absence, your wife is the absolute boss.

8. You are a small, selfish, helpless moron, incapable of thought or opinion. To attempt to think otherwise is an affront to God and your fellows who are trying to save you.

9. The only reactions to a suggestion are yes, I understand, and yes, I do not understand and need clarification.

B. Work

1. Become willing to do whatever is needed, to be of value to others.

2. Eliminate any notion of what you want in a job, or what you "relate" to.

3. Be willing to work hard.

4. Be willing to travel, and to never see your family.

5. Be willing to relocate anywhere in the world.

6. Become willing to re-train (e.g. for a medical degree).

7. Sign up to run a charity marathon.

8. Help another job seeker with their resume.

9. Be willing to sell.

10. Be willing to work for no pay.

11. Identify people who have the money and authority to hire and go see them. Make an appointment, if necessary. Just go.

12. Identify all companies in your area and go visit them personally. See what they do, find out their problems, and see how you can ease their pain.

13. Find pain in your community and solve it.

14. Find pain with a potential employer and help solve it for free, or at least enough to demonstrate the value of having you around.

15. Develop a visceral, automatic reaction of helpfulness to those that can help you. Take it further. Be that way to everyone. The only thing that should restrict your effort is whether it diverts your service to another. Your needs and preferences should be of no concern.

16. Find an established, successful marketing expert or acclaimed member of your professional area. Go see them personally. Ask that person to tell you what makes up an excellent job search. Then do exactly that.

17. On the job, continue your quest for helpfulness.

18. For security, become vital. Strengthen your ties to the revenue source.

19. Make others look good. Develop a "bank" of goodwill. At some point, everyone ends up wishing they had done this more. Even if there is no crisis, the friendships developed will come to be cherished.

20. Be generous in your service and your time .

21. Pray. A lot. Develop an ongoing conversation and relationship with God.

Be humble. Submit to God. Let His strength, His confidence, and His grace flow through you. Minimize all things that are you, your pride, your ego, your vanity, your arrogance, and your will.

Beat back your tendencies to re-inflate yourself, especially when the crisis dies down, and you are not in such desperate need. That is easy to say, but very hard to do. Be humble, and release the Holy Spirit within you.

Chapter Twelve

Responsibility

For most of us, responsibility is an ongoing chore. But what is it exactly? Could it be just what it says, the "ability to respond?" Are we being asked to willingly take appropriate action when needed? What could be so hard about that?

Have you ever heard the statement, "It is easy when it is easy?" For me, reality does not seem to care whether it is easy or not. It just is what it is. The pleasantness of the task is usually up to me and is determined by how I approach it.

My parents tried to teach me many lessons that I ended up having to learn myself, very often the hard way. It took me a long time to truly internalize that I will eventually have to answer for everything. So I might as well do things as best I can now, for there are eventual rewards or consequences for shoddy behavior, mediocre behavior, and excellence.

This simple, unavoidable tie between current behavior and future consequences has been taught to me well (do I see my second grade teacher smiling along with my parents?). It is very helpful for me to keep reminding myself of this. Even so, I do not always practice it, as the "forgetter" in my head is extremely well-developed. But I do things regularly to keep me exposed to its reality.

We have very little control over the timing of outcomes. My inability to control the timing of consequences often fueled my denial. I had to understand and remember that timing is in God's hands, but the consequences are in mine.

Accountability is good. Many forward thinking people I've met deliberately structure accountability in their lives. Despite the awkward inconvenience, they are self-aware enough to appreciate the eventual benefits. Everyone has some tendency to avoid the reality of their own irresponsibility. We all must take deliberate steps to counter this decay.

Gradually we learn that what is inconvenient or difficult today can become horrendous if ignored. At the same time, we must not try to solve problems that aren't there. Nor should we deny future consequences to justify behavior today. That takes a wisdom, balance, and judgment that elude most of us.

* * * *

Business success can be elusive. Everyone wants it.
In a competitive industry, I have had to learn to stand up for
my enterprise, whether I liked it or not. I had to because
I'm responsible for supporting five people, and I know that
is what God wants me to do. He makes it possible, but he
doesn't make it easy!

In December, 2003, a young man came to me
wondering how to make it in business. I wrote:

> *"I want you to think hard about what is
> required to be an owner/equity partner in
> business. Not that you cannot do it, but you have
> to realize what mental equipment and skills you
> need to develop or acquire. For example, think
> about your last situation. A business owner needs
> to have the skills to correct the situation.
> Knowledge of facts is important, but it is not that
> important. Experience and judgment are far more
> important. Most owners, for example, know their
> finances intuitively.*
>
> *They understand cash flow and appreciate
> its importance, particularly revenue. If you are a
> cost center, you will never have financial security.
> Frequently, people fail because they cannot think
> like owners. What are you good at? What will
> cause people to give their hard earned money to
> you? More importantly, what critical areas of*

> *business have you failed to develop because you*
> *didn't like them?"*

I pray to God every day to lend me some of His wisdom and strength. In return, He lifts a little of the haze of human confusion and self-centeredness, giving me a little clarity to get by.

* * * * *

When faced with a big decision, one where the consequences seem to be great, I try to look at it from a different perspective. This is especially useful where I could make a mistake with either choice, and the consequences of either mistake would be costly.

If my analysis of the potential benefits from the alternatives does not produce a clear choice, I turn it around and analyze the relative consequences. Which risk can I better endure? Should you let your teenager take the car out alone for the first time? You could make the mistake of giving him the privilege too early, in which case the consequences would be serious. Or, you could wait until he is ready to handle the responsibility. At least to me, the choice becomes vivid.

For example, your child (or you) does not want to wear a bike safety helmet because it looks "dorky". If you don't wear it but end up needing it, the consequences could be tragic. If you do wear it, and someone thinks you are less than stylish, this becomes a lesser downside. My teenagers, however, may think both of these risks are equally anguishing. I find myself being wrapped up in silly, shallow considerations all the time. It is helpful to be able to stop, pray, and get my mind right.

* * * * *

We have a responsibility to God. We need to prepare and conduct ourselves so that our fellows can depend on us, and we must depend on God to do it. Many of His gifts are delivered to us by others around us. We need each other, but we cannot expect others to bear a burden for us that God wants us to bear ourselves.

In my case, He seems to make the burden so great that no one else would even think of taking it on (I probably would let someone just to get out from under it), and then I have to pray and pray. Eventually, I end up growing to the point where I can and will handle it, usually in some painful process I'll try to avoid in the future, and maybe tell others so they can just skip that step.

Often times fierce independence, for example from God, results in tragedy. Many times we overestimate our ability to act independently of God, thinking we can take responsibility for things we cannot control. We end up in a pickle, and then have to reach out in desperation to a person or thing that ends up disappointing us.

When I was growing up, I developed a fierce need for independence. The bold, adventuresome, self–reliant heroes of both history and film fueled my zeal for doing things my way, on my terms. James Bond, George Washington, Hugh Hefner, Albert Einstein, and Elvis Presley were not famed for being whiny, needy dependents. They were our childhood heroes.

My father was also fiercely independent, but for the noble goal of never wanting to be a burden to others. The attraction to me was being able to make your own rules, at least on the surface.

Trying to grasp the idea that dependence on God was both noble and powerful, certainly more so than any other independence, was beyond my spiritual capacity. I later had to learn that <u>more</u> dependence on God resulted in <u>less</u> dependence on your fellows, and therefore, more independence here on earth.

* * * * *

Once my mind found more and more truth, I was able to accept that many important realities are paradoxes, and not obvious ones. Many are subtle, but many more are intriguingly counter-intuitive. Unless you have had a certain level of experience to counter the obvious, or deep faith in a source that you trust against your own instincts, it is impossible to know these.

There are many paradoxical concepts I've learned in my own recovery that I am surprised I didn't pick up earlier. That is because there are many people who did pick them up early, or went ahead and trusted a source (an example is Proverbs). They didn't go through a lot of the painful experience I endured in order to plant these lessons in my thick skull. I have a great deal more respect for these people, and I congratulate their foresight. I listen a lot more now, and study these matters. It has helped my life become much more manageable and productive.

Here are some of my favorite, most useful, rediscovered paradoxes:

Surrender can win when nothing else will.

Patience is quicker than impatience.

To truly feel better physically, go to a gym and hurt until you feel better.

Good works won't get you into heaven.

Serve others to help yourself.

Willingness to do what you don't want to do, often means you won't have to do it.

> *Dependence on God results in independence from man.*

And so on. Email me yours!

Galaxies of other important truths begin to emerge as you dig deeper. They are only hidden by our shallow need to understand everything immediately, so we are easily blinded by matters that will eventually be obvious. We develop an "irrational admiration of the rational."

This limits us to microscopic portions of reality. We miss much of what we need to know to manage and survive in our world.

It is our responsibility, to God, to ourselves, and our fellows, to constantly dig for the truth, and use it in service to all.

Chapter Thirteen

Maintaining Spiritual Fitness

It is hard to maintain a good spiritual condition. Like a car, I have to invest in maintenance or I degrade. While I've come to enjoy most of these activities, I didn't necessarily enjoy them in the beginning, but I did them anyway. If things changed and I began to dislike them, I still did them. It is actually irrelevant whether I enjoy them or not. I've come to accept that the world does not revolve around my personal preferences. That is reality. While good things can be pleasurable, they never necessarily are. The further I get from giving any weight to my personal perspective, the better off I am.

After I let go of doing things the way I prefer or according to my prescription, these matters take on less weight and my reluctance and complacency recede. This is like exercise, where you must do something you don't necessarily enjoy now to be able to have a greater reward later. Denzel Washington once said, "You must do what you have to do, to be able to do what you want to do."

In hindsight, it's easy to see our reluctance so clearly. Despite being 53 years old, I have to fight a childish desire to only do what I want to do, when I want to do it. I should know better, but my mind needs to be trained, and constantly reminded, that thinking and acting like an adult will bring me more eventual good, than acting like a child.

I believe I have self-centeredness hard-wired in me. There will always be a part of me that wants instant gratification in the form of personal pleasure. I think all humans have this to some degree. In fact, we might all have it to the same degree. There is not one person yet who has told me they have never had to deal with personal temptation. It is our spiritual condition that keeps us from giving way to this ever present tendency. Everyone has different levels of desire and the ability to quell it.

Having the terrible and gut-wrenching memories of my active addiction gives me a vivid, personal example of what happens when I give full way to my baser instincts. I was given the opportunity and resources to carry my selfishness to whatever degree I wanted.

Paradoxically, my selfish quest almost killed me, and it didn't give me the physical comfort and pleasure I sought. It took from me. It gave me cold, steel drunk tanks and dirty, pounding hangovers. It gave me embarrassed children, and brought shame. It destroyed me. I have seen the same pattern hundreds of times, because I've opened my eyes to the reality of life.

Once I was taught not to follow most of my instincts, I began to feel other instincts when people actually said "go ahead." In those early days, and to a great degree still, I relied on others to tell me if my personal plans were good or bad. This usually came from my wife, my sponsor, or my doctor, but increasingly it came from friends and fellows whom I admired and who had a good, moral, and well-developed code of behavior. Sometimes my mind can't distinguish between what is good or bad for me. While I am learning and can now make a lot of these decisions myself, it is only from hearing it from other people so many times that I can inherently know what they would say. When I think "maybe I'll stop for ice cream" when I should be headed to the carpool line to pick up a child from school, I can pretty much bet my wife would tell me, "no, pick up your son, and then <u>both</u> of you go for ice cream."

I learned this only by asking her what to do in many situations over and over. It seemed to be childish and hurt my ego that I had to ask other's opinions on so many matters. However, I had to learn that what I thought about the situation did not matter, and that it would probably be wrong. This was very humbling, but consequently, it increased my spiritual condition, so I continued to do it.

Once I began to improve my behavioral decision-making by internalizing the judgment and wisdom of others, I noticed that not every notion I had involved self-seeking gratification. A lot did, and still does, but not all. I actually started to want to do something nice for someone else. Early on I had the strong feeling that my family deserved better. The idea began to grow that I should stay clean not only for myself, but that being a good father and husband would do a world of good for the family I had disrespected and neglected for so long. It was the start of many spiritual inklings.

It wasn't always easy to follow these inklings. First, they were not that apparent, being dominated by my more base desires. With spiritual maintenance, however, they became clearer over time. My awareness, specifically my spiritual awareness, increased as I put more work into it.

Secondly, it is more socially correct, especially in the U.S., to be continuously focused on a plan of action, to use a To Do list, or something similar, that delivers an obvious goal. The goals of spiritual inklings are usually not obvious, unless one is exceptionally developed. Therefore, they can be easily dismissed as flights of fancy to be avoided, or as diversions from our sacred action plans that we execute with such dispatch. Here are some personal examples.

While on vacation on Amelia Island in 2004, I applied for membership in an Episcopal church and made a small contribution. I keep my membership at home, but this idea came to me during one of my frequent visits to their beautiful chapel.

Joining this church was an inkling. I felt I needed to be more a part of this congregation in which I had been led to pray for the last several years while on vacation. I tended to get up early, before the family rose for their day of activity, and wander about the island in the early morning hours, enjoying the beauty, the serenity, the quiet, and the independence.

Part of this church's spiritual exercise is to conduct a twice weekly morning prayer and meditation time. I was told of it by the assistant rector of this beautiful antebellum sanctuary. I had stopped in to pray on a Wednesday afternoon, as the bright summer sun streamed through the wonderful stained glass window. The church was narrow, the roof high and pitched, like many old European cathedrals. An air of nobility hung in the wooden buttressing that enticed one's respectful gaze heavenward. No wonder they had pillows and kneeling rails. Prayer seemed to be the most natural thing to do. I could feel the moving presence of our Savior. He was with me.

When no one is there, in the cool morning of summer, you can walk up to the front, past the pulpit, past the choir benches, to stand directly in front of the giant stained glass figures of Saint Peter, Saint Paul, and in the middle, Jesus, holding a lamb with a white dove flying above him. Kneeling before these icons, one is comfortably facing east. So in the early hours of the day, the sun is shining through the windows, bursting through in a brilliant montage of color.

That morning, the sun was at Christ's feet. But as I supplicated myself in soft reverence, praying for the ability to see His will and His light, and to remove my thoughts and replace them with His, the sun slowly rose up the image of Christ to where it stood directly behind his face, his golden halo filling the cathedral and my heart with his wondrous favor.

I was glad I got up!

Most spiritual maintenance is not glamorous, but it need not be burdensome either. Attitude improvement, which usually accompanies it, vastly improves the experience. Like exercise, it may seem like a pain until you get going, but once you do, you forget about your initial reluctance. How many things are like that? My first sponsor told me "you don't have to have willingness before you take action. In many cases you take the indicated action, and the willingness will follow." How true! Sometimes I wander by a sink full of dirty dishes thinking I had better get to those, but I don't feel willing at the time. However, once I actually start and realize it is only going to take a few minutes and it will be done, I wonder why I was so reluctant in the first place. You would think the next time the sink was full I would remember this lesson, but I don't. Same old reluctance, same old "taking action" even though I don't feel it when I am initiating the action.

There is a lot in my life that is like that sink of dishes. Part of my growing up was not only recognizing what needed to be cleaned up, but taking the action to get it done before I felt the willingness to start. Reluctance and complacency are deadly.

You have to learn to do it, no matter how you happen to feel about it at the time. Trust me, it pays off. In fact, attitude improvement follows spiritual improvement in "lock-step" in most cases, not to mention the whole panoply of dividends overall.

I developed a series of simple things to do on a regular basis to maintain and improve my spiritual condition. My spirituality, and I suspect many other people's, is like a bathtub with the drain open, always in decline unless fed. My natural human condition is to drift away from God. Thank goodness I go to enough meetings to now know the cost of that complacency. For us alcoholics and drug addicts it is a deadly issue. We <u>have</u> to maintain to keep our heads above water. I suspect that for those to whom it is not a deadly matter, they simply drift in an essentially Godless existence of self-control, and self-seeking. And because their only pain may be the emptiness, anxiety, and the burden of shouldering responsibility they can never keep, they lead bland lives of quiet desperation.

My routine is very doable. It takes very little time if I am pushed, but it can be expanded to fit however much time I am called to put into it. I pray for God to allow me to recognize how much time I need to put into spiritual matters and to do them. In fact, that fits nicely into Step 11. "Seek through prayer and meditation to improve my conscious contact with God, praying only for the knowledge of his will for me and the power to carry it out."

That is far harder than it looks, to pray *only* to do God's will. Intellectually, I can see how that is meant to show me that doing God's will is all that is needed to be able and willing to do, but I am just not there yet spiritually. Someday, I hope.

Consequently, I don't miss morning prayer. I slide out of bed by first swinging my legs over the side, while lying on my stomach, face down. Then I slide off the bed, onto my knees in one simple motion. While I'm in this position, I say the Serenity prayer, which is short, and then recite the 12 steps up to the one I am working on. In the beginning this was a very short exercise. Serenity prayer plus Step 1...done. That's all. It was so easy I couldn't believe it. Now I go through the entire 12 steps, so I know them by heart, and they have crossed my mind before I do anything else. I do add on whatever else I may want to pray about. Today it was thanking God for allowing me such a wonderful family, and for keeping them healthy and giving them and my wife a life they seem to enjoy. I also thanked him for letting me actually wake up, as that did not necessarily have to happen.

Then I'm on to the bathroom and on to work,

grateful that I have work to go to, and that I have many things, and many comforts. I'm <u>so</u> grateful that I pray I won't screw this up, or misbehave in a way that makes God think I need a little message or reminder (I hate those). And I go to a meeting every chance I get, usually two to three a week.

Now, you would think this would be enough. But it isn't. There is one more thing so insidious and subtle that it took other people to warn me. That is the critical element of self-correction.

This is to realize that no matter how well you think you're doing, you always have to be taking action, because we are all just treading water. To an athlete, this is well understood. But they have peer pressure and visible physical deterioration that makes their complacency so obvious, it can be corrected. With the element of denial, particularly in recovery but also true elsewhere, one doesn't realize they are slipping away and their spiritual condition is decaying until something bad slams them in the head. I had to develop a habit of constantly re-energizing my spiritual maintenance program just to stay safe. Despite how arduous that may sound, one gets used to it, others will encourage and respect you for it, and the rewards are enormous.

Here are some exercises I use to keep me spiritually strong. They are easy to do and are particularly revealing of our human inabilities. I have to remind myself that where there is pain, there is usually a spiritual growth opportunity.

1) Fight Temptation.

> We humans fight a losing battle against sin everyday. But it is in this battle that we win our lives with Christ. It is not in winning, because we cannot. It is preparing and fighting the cause that brings us the spiritual reward.

> I recently heard someone on the radio describe our dilemma of the flesh this way. "Why fight a war that has already been lost, when we should accept the victory that has already been won."

> We need to go to God in prayer, to ask that he remove the temptation we cannot remove ourselves, and commit ourselves to doing as He wants.

2) Before taking action, run the idea by others.

3) Pray whenever and wherever it crosses your mind.

4) Read the Bible, noting all of the timeless wisdom.

5) Be grateful.

6) Help others.

7) Exercise, be quiet, and listen. Meditate.

When I run long distances, I become tired and achy well before I'm half way through, and I want to stop. If I

stop, and just walk, my whole body will relax, I will breathe
normally, and enjoy the great physical feeling of having run
whatever distance I have up to that point. But I can't fall for
that trap. Once stopped, I won't want to start back. My
muscles will burn, my neck will cramp and my breathing
will become labored. Time and distance go by ever so
slowly. I can hear that voice in my head. "Lee, take it easy.
Just stop for a minute. You deserve it. No one else is even
out here. No one is looking. Everyone else has stopped.
You have already outdone everybody. You're already slow,
why not stop and walk?"

There is always the temptation to stop. To be free of
this discomfort, I don't have to <u>do</u> anything. I'm actively
inflicting pain on myself. The temptation is to simply <u>*not*</u>
keep doing it.

I have to practice putting one foot in front of the
other, despite the pain and my flesh's demands. Each step
is an exercise in resistance to immediate gratification. The
payoff comes when I finish the run. When I make it, I
receive a substantial reward. Interestingly, these rewards
include more physical pleasure than I could have ever
achieved by stopping before the end. Here are some of
these rewards:

1) The immediate physical relief from the
   immediate pain we were enduring;
2) The cumulative pleasure from all of those

individual steps, where a decision was made not to stop, and the pleasure deferred;

3) The satisfaction of achievement;

4) An even greater level of physical comfort throughout the rest of the day;

5) Sounder sleep that night;

6) Better health in general;

7) The knowledge you have defeated short-term temptation for a longer-term greater good.

Again, there is the paradox—invest in temporary discomfort for greater long term rewards. Here we could draw a parallel to many life events, for example, saving for retirement. We give up something on a regular basis for a greater payoff down the road.

This exercise can be done thousands of times, over and over, every time we take a positive step where the payoff is not immediate. It reveals to me how short-sighted, immediate, and self-centered I really am. Even in this exercise, the payoff is to me.

I gain even more respect for those that give up immediate comfort for the long term benefit of others. They run painful steps and then handoff the reward to others. That is a level of selflessness worth emulating.

There are even those that go beyond this and simply do it for the pleasure of Christ. And then there is Christ himself, who gave his life, quite painfully, so that God could justly give us, his selfish sinners, abundant life on earth, and eternity.

But our egos make it difficult to see beyond the immediate cost or inconvenience.

Throughout the day, I often notice how my perception of myself can change from hero to knucklehead and back with ease. When playing golf, I am always amazed at my ego's ability to change my entire view of myself based on the golf shot I just made. Hit a good shot and all of a sudden I'm a little bit younger, a little slimmer, and a little wiser. I walk down the fairway confident, a player, a man in control of his destiny. Shortly thereafter, I'll flub a shot, and I'm an old hack, awkward, old, and kidding himself that I could even pretend to be anything resembling an athlete.

And so it goes, back and forth. It's all meaningless ego. When we can ignore it, and come to laugh at it, we draw closer to the ability to see things from God's perspective, not our own, and thus strengthen our spiritual condition.

Chapter Fourteen

Prayer

The very first action I took in recovery was to pray. In rehab and in lockdown, I had no choice but to not use drugs and to follow directions. But I knew that once the "heat" was off, even a little, it would be hard for me to keep vigilant in any recovery program. I prayed frequently for the willingness to do what I was told to do to stay clean when I was unsupervised.

Prayer is not explicitly addressed in 12 step programs until late in the process. This is because it takes at least the ten preceding recovery steps to cultivate the clarity to understand the urgency of an unhurried submission to God in prayer. It is another paradox.

In addiction recovery, the first three steps are sometimes characterized as "I can't, He can, I will let Him." The fourth and fifth examine one's past harms and expunge them. Released from the past to the present, Steps 6 and 7 allow one to be truthfully aware of the world and oneself, and require the willingness and humility to submit to unnatural behavior, i.e., "to remove all my defects of character", not just some defects, <u>all</u>. Very important, this. Steps 8, 9, and 10 describe the ongoing cycle of making amends for our never-ending transgressions (though with work they should diminish), and to make it a daily habit to review our behavior and self-correct when necessary (Step 10). Whew, that's a lot of work! It took me about five years to thoroughly work the first ten steps.

After all of this, Step 11 brought a new surprise, at least it was to me.

"Sought through prayer and meditation to improve my conscious contact with God, as I understand him, praying only for the knowledge of His Will for me, and the power to carry it out."

News flash: Everything I had learned so far, everything I needed to know or do about anything, can be summarized by simply knowing and doing God's will. This isn't easy. Try it. Literally get down on your knees to pray, and instead of the usual long list of items we need help with, pray to know God's will for you and have the willingness to do it. Then stop and get up. That's all that is necessary. Everything we have been working on so far, and will ever do in the future, falls under the vast umbrella of this simple, short, life-changing notion.

I have heard prayer divided into praise, submission,

healing, and intercessory prayer. We pray to remove ourselves for a few moments from the mortal to the holy. We are able to speak directly with God and to develop our own personal relationship with Him. No one will hear what we ask or the nature of our conversation. This is such an incredible privilege that I have to laugh/cry at my own irreverence at how I don't take advantage of this gift as I should, how I abuse it, and give it short shrift. But it is there for all, and there is no one to tell us whether our prayers are answered. Only we and God know what we asked, and only we know if our prayer is truly answered.

I can say from experience that I would not pray if there were no answer. I no longer do it because I'm told to or because it is accepted and allows me to cull the benefits by conforming to a "group think" that prayer is wonderful. Nobody knows if I pray, and they certainly don't know what is said when I do. I do it because of the results. I do it because I need things that are far larger than me, that can only be accomplished by divine intervention.

One of these things is simply keeping myself in His will, and not fighting to take back control, or develop the deadly disease of self-reliance.

Many of us parents have found how little actual control we have over things, risks, and realities that affect the children we love. We go to God to protect them, and to mold us, that we might be able to raise them with peace, reverence, and joy in a dangerous world of superficial distractions and traps.

Prayer is so simple, we find it hard to accept as seasoned, worldly adults. Most of my life I thought about prayer as a juvenile exercise for those too weak to go out into the world and achieve whatever they wanted. It seemed like a child making out a birthday wish list for parents. In fact, it wasn't too long after discovering the truth behind Santa Claus did I conclude that God and Christ were the same type of mythical, fictional inventions of infantile minds.

But the ugly end product of my brilliant worldliness was self-centered obsession locked in a mental hospital's detox ward. So who is the child here? When you are out of options, look at what others are doing. Go with what works.

Many adults, and I dare say millions, kneel before God everyday, but bow to no man, and they don't care what it looks like to others. These are not people that pray just because their parents require it, nor is it to blend in with their peers. They do it in private. But if you never go to church, you may never get to see it. There are many, many people who pray forcefully, even zealously, because of their own real experience that it works. It brings them relief and comfort to know that they have discovered a great adult truth of life hidden behind the appearance of something so child-like that lesser intellects often dismiss it as fantasy.

When I first wandered into the Church, I had about two years clean, a fair amount of time, and I was feeling much better physically. I began to rediscover a friendly, sunnier side to me that had been hidden for years. In active addiction, I had become isolative, moody, and paranoid. Without chemicals, the real me re-emerged.

All my life, I have been blessed with many friends. When I began to attend church, I was happy to meet and be welcomed by many gracious people. They encouraged me and were patient with my many questions.

All I had was the ability to be respectful and curious. By this time I knew these "church people" were also parents and workers and had problems just like me. I remember looking down the long prayer request list at one of my first services to see all of the names and maladies the church published weekly, so that members could pray for those in need.

As I scanned down the list I remember seeing "cancer", "teenager in coma", "find Daddy a job", "son killed in Iraq", and so on.

These were not requests of sunny, rich pollyannas. These were real people who were beaten to their knees, crying out from their anguish for help. These were brave people who only asked for prayers and understanding from a congregation that took time to look at the dirty, ugly side of things, and throw it out for all to see.

These people were not shirking reality, they were accepting responsibility and dealing with it. They had the guts to show that all is not well in paradise and that the world is hard and cruel.

That gave me real pause. Here I was thinking that these were all well positioned, happy people with no problems. I had been comparing their "outsides" to my "insides" without having the respect to get to know them as individuals. That gave me an entirely new, respectful perspective. I began to think of the congregation as more honest, everyday people, who had big enough problems to be driven to each other and to God to solve, because problems could get that big and often did. Just like me. Just like me.

I was also curious. What was it that drove everyone? When did they discover this adult form of belief in Christ? I learned that everyone was different. There was no formula, and if someone had survived to reach the age of forty, almost every one of them had a story to tell of hardship, of long periods without God, of having to face and overcome horrifying circumstance. Yet it all brought them here, on their knees, to beg like children for the continued grace of God.

My first prayers in rehab were to give me the willingness to do whatever I needed to do to stay off drugs. I didn't know if it would work, of course, but I had been told to pray for this. At some point in those first few weeks I put forth a fundamental problem. I could easily lose the desire to stay clean. How do you stay clean when you don't want to? Even with all the consequences you know too well, with all the promises and training and lamenting, an addict can often just tune all that out and want to use.

For that, I was told to go to God. All of the greatest medicine and therapy in the world cannot affect that miracle. Especially for me. I leaned over the side of my bed, unsure and uncomfortable, and quietly asked, "God, fill me with desire to not use, to be a good husband and father, and to sustain the willingness to follow directions and do whatever I need to do to stay clean. Amen". I was alone. It was private.

Now, September 17, 2007, I am eight days away from having ten years clean. *Ten years clean.* Journal entry: September 25, 2007. I made it! Ten rich years I don't deserve, but I have anyway.

Was my prayer answered? Did I receive the willingness I needed at first? Did I become a good husband and father that I asked to be?

You will have to ask my wife and kids for sure, but I think they will agree that at least I have been average, or maybe a little above. I certainly have been light years ahead of the sociopathic nightmare I was steering them towards in active addiction.

Many of the people in the meetings of recovery had parents that were addicts and alcoholics. Not only is there a genetic link, but the dangerous, neglectful, cruel environment of an impaired parent can cause many mental problems later in life.

One of my most cherished, and completely unexpected rewards of recovery has been the reflection of my recovery and spiritual program in my children's lives. Even just an average clean parent provides an incredibly important stability for children from which they can learn to manage their lives. It also seems that having seen a parent attending Church and praying openly on a daily basis tells the children how serious the parent is about spiritual matters. When they see themselves, or better yet their schoolmates, getting into trouble from immaturity or naïveté, they have an example of what one beat-up adult has learned to lean on—prayer on a regular basis.

My guess is that God helped me raise my kids, of whom I am so proud of today. I am not proud of what I did, which was to take a stab in the dark as to what was right and try not to get too off-track. God asked me to keep an eye out for anything lethal, criminal, or cruel as best I could. He kept them from danger, he brought learning from those painful growing adjustments, he brought the team football that developed many life helping traits in my son, and allowed my daughter to grow up alongside horses, which taught her confidence, accountability, and savvy far beyond her years. My youngest son Langdon is perhaps the most like me. He has not received as much materially as the first two, but he has developed into one of the brightest kids I have ever met.

So far (knock on wood), I could not ask for more.

Somehow I have been able to let my wife stay at home while I provided the support. If you have read this far you will realize this has been far from easy, to keep a regular supply of cash coming in to support five people, and no circumstance and no excuses allowed. Every month, the same hurdle. You lost your job? Too bad, find the money. Your business collapses, you owe $800,000? Marshals are serving lawsuits to your door? Too bad, find the money. You can only get a job paying $8,000 less per month than your family needs? Too bad, get the money. Your new business needs advertising, you can't borrow, the Church needs your pledge, and your kid needs a football helmet? Too bad, you have to come up with the money.

No one on earth goes through that unless they have to. It is mind numbing, but you know what? You can get through it. And, like many other things, there is an enormous unexpected benefit. You adapt. You learn to do your duty under fire. If the commitment is there, it will get done. If it is God's will, it will be done. And you can be the one to do it.

What do you do when you are really in the soup? When each alternative is horrible, you have no resources, no ideas, no help, no experience, and you want to be out of this situation, but it keeps getting worse?

You pray. That's what you do, pray.

When I finally blew through that last $300,000 I borrowed to keep my business open and was no closer to stemming the tide of the money I was losing, I had to decide. Should I close the business? Is there a saving deal out there next week if I hang in there or am I finished? And what is "finished", exactly? By closing the business, I would have no job at all, and no income. But zero income was better than losing $150,000 per year.

So I prayed. Hard. What was I supposed to do? And if I did close my business, what then? I knew God had a plan for me, and I realized that I wanted to stop self-inflicting pain. I hate pain, and most of it is self-inflicted. The only thing I knew to do was to go ahead and do exactly what God wanted me to, no matter what I thought about it personally. If that meant becoming a garbage man, so be it. I had to become willing to do anything, just like we were taught in recovery. Let go, and let God.

In my opinion, the only good way to understand God better is through prayer. I did a lot of praying, in the office, stopping by the Church on weekdays, by my bed, as much as I could.

I found that 1) he wanted me to continue to be a good husband and father, therefore, I wasn't to use or drink no matter what, and 2) I should use my experience, training, and small corpus of clients to re-start my career by going to work in a giant firm's training program! Arghh! How humiliating! But that is what he said. And finally, He told me that He wanted me to pay off all my debts and for my family to live an abundant life. I was glad to hear that until

I found out what He wanted me to do. I was to take stock of myself, here and now, broke, and get ready to take a trainee's salary, and I was to develop the skills to become valuable enough that others would pay me enough to pay off my debts, and to be the husband, father, and man that I could be. That way, He explained, I would never have to worry about money for my family again. It would take care of the issue once and for all. It would take everything I had learned to this point and more. It would take more patience and understanding and hard work than I had ever known. But there were to be no more temporary windfalls, no more stocks that brought instant wealth, or business ventures that "take off." No, this is going to be a slow and steady trudge uphill. No matter what was put in front of me, no matter how complex or delicate the situation, I would have the skills and experience to be a productive element of the solution. I would be productive and valuable enough to pay for my past and future costs, and those of my family. And I was to no longer possess anything.

Everything I made would be given away to someone else. I was to be an empty vessel, a productive catalyst that woke up everyday and had something to eat by the grace of God.

I knelt down again, and prayed even more. I prayed for the wisdom and patience and perseverance to carry out this task, to be what he called me to be, and to do what He wanted me to do. All the lessons I had learned this far were to be focused into even more learning. What I thought about it did not matter at all. How I looked doing it did not matter at all. I knew that I was on thin ice, and if I became the least bit proud or too relaxed, I would receive a prompt dose of humility to put me in my place. I could do it the easy way or the hard way, but the rest of my life would be played out God's way.

I started down His path as best as I could see it. Using prayer and meditation to guide me, I stumbled into the light.

Chapter Fifteen

Spiritual Awakening

As I write this on July 4th, 2006, I think it would be appropriate to say something about independence on the 230th birthday of our nation.

I am looking out over the Amelia River, in Northeast Florida, at 8 a.m. on the July 4th holiday. I have my laptop plugged into my car, and my car is perched up on a sand bluff with the warm sun slowly rising to my back.

We are on holiday and my family is sleeping back at the condo. I like to wake a few hours before everyone, get in my car and go exploring for that first great cup of island espresso. With ice water in the cup holder, I seek out the most beautiful and tranquil place I can find and drink in the beauty and quiet and uniqueness of God's creation. For many years I would awaken here with a giant, killer hangover and completely miss what is now my most cherished time of day.

I have already prayed this morning. In fact, I do it so routinely now that I actually repeated the Serenity prayer and 12 steps by rote, as my mind wandered to something else. I had to start over. Now is not the time to give short shrift to God. My wife and youngest son, who crawled into our king-sized bed sometime in the night, snoozed angelically as I slipped out the door. They will be able to sleep for hours more and be grateful for it. I get to be a kid again, roaming the island in the cool morning air like a serene buccaneer before most people are up.

We have been coming to this island for a week at the beach for fifteen years. If I am eight years clean, that leaves seven years when I wasn't here. I, and everyone else, have vivid, awful memories of those times, of my embarrassing, dangerous, and child-like actions that shamed everyone. It is a great time to reflect on what freedom and independence have come to mean to me.

Independence to me is enjoying this morning without heart pounding guilt about what I did last night.

It is:

Knowing my wife and children are not only happy, but delighted to be here.

Knowing my wife will wake, and seeing me gone, will not fear for my life, or the family's existence.

The freedom to change, such as liking exercise, water, and even some healthy foods.

The freedom to make friends with just about anyone I meet.

The freedom that comes from knowing that almost everything I will ever have will come from outside me, usually in the form of someone else, and that if I am more pleasant, respectful, and understanding, I will receive pleasant surprises from others.

The freedom to be the husband I promised to be. Like fatherhood, the enormous joy returned to me for this is something I never could have understood until it happened. Luckily, I have been around, and am around all the time, guys who see this, and help encourage each other when we tend to forget it.

Today, I enjoy the:

Freedom to know there are a few prohibited actions that will destroy me, but I may pursue the other ninety-nine percent of life with gusto.

Freedom to read, and to learn, anything.

Freedom that comes from the respect of others.

Freedom and confidence and well-being that comes from respecting oneself.

Freedom to be of value to others, thousands of others, who suffer.

Freedom to love, and to be loved.

Freedom to choose your friends, and to be enough of a value as a friend to be desired as a friend.

Freedom to have the faith to utilize less than obvious paths of action, which is most of the actions required for significant result.

* * * *

It was my youngest son, Langdon, 13 years old, who asked, completely unexpectedly, to speak aloud to a grizzled group of forty recovering addicts at my home group just after my wife had presented me with my ten year medallion. He had dressed in a coat and tie.

He was only two at the time I gave up the fight. "I really cannot remember those times when I was a baby," he eloquently began. "But I have been reading parts of a book my Dad has been writing about those times, and I want to say how happy I am that he and you have found this new way to live. I am glad to have a father in recovery and I'm glad my Daddy didn't die when I was a baby. I love him. Thank you."

And an entire room let loose a tear. To all the newcomers in the room that night, and to all of those struggling to find a reason to hang on and get past those terrible early days of not using, my son presented one of the greatest gifts recovery and the Grace of God can give, the life, safety, happiness, gratitude, and respect of one's child.

As the evil tentacles of addiction infect every crevice of self, family, and community, so does the illuminating light of God raise up with love and restore those ties among us, with power to build far greater than evil's power to destroy.

* * * *

The entire rehab therapy and treatment is based on groups. This is no accident. Most patients come in like I did, isolated loners, no matter what disposition they would normally have. Addiction does that.

Being in a group, while way beyond my understanding at the time, was part of the necessary re-entry into life. Man is a social animal.

After rehab, the first awkward groups I reluctantly made myself a part of (after Ridgeview enthusiastically made me a part of) were recovery groups. This saved my life and has for millions of others.

I didn't see them as having anything I could relate to, at least not at first. But it was the only option for me to have even a remote hope of staying clean for my drug tests; if failed, I was automatically sent to prison.

As I began to jog more and more, I noticed my running acquaintances were usually "cool", especially in areas of pettiness and being "heavy". They were also really patient with me. Running with them became, dare I say it, enjoyable.

While in training with the Leukemia Society for my

first marathon, I noticed how little pettiness there was among the volunteer runners. As a charity event, I think now it attracts a certain type of giving individual. Most have had some personal experience with cancer, a loved one or themselves, and I think this creates a more respectful, grateful person. It also doesn't hurt to have seven year-old cancer patients manning the water stations, with their parents nearby, to thank you for running the event because your efforts are saving their children. I thought I was only trying to get a little faster running a 10k. This was something else. It was also *real*. These parents weren't blowing smoke. We were saving lives.

Traveling with a group of marathoners was a great experience, especially to a place like Bermuda. I never expected this. To me, I always thought those joggers were merciless, boring, sweaty masochists because that was all I saw from my car or living room window. I was quite ready to smugly judge those I had no experience with or knew anything about. A wonderful thing that had been slowly developing in me was the reluctance to judge others. I realized that it was better to respectfully get to know people, or groups, or almost anything first if you absolutely *must* form an opinion at all.

* * * *

I was initially drawn to the Masonic Lodge by a

tremendous curiosity. Who were these guys? I wanted to find out and I had no idea why.

I had passed the Lodge in our town many times, but this time there were a number of cars parked outside, with much activity inside. What the heck? Apprehensively, I went up and knocked on the door.

It turns out this is the exact way that men become Masons. One must seek out Masonry out of one's own curiosity and respect. No one is invited. It is up to each man, and God, to be led to the Lodge door.

Once there, it takes another leap of faith to go through the months' long learning and initiation process without ever knowing what goes on inside a Masonic Lodge meeting. You cannot be in a meeting of Master Masons (the third degree) unless you *are* a Master Mason. It takes a lot of work, including trials and tests in front of the members, before you are even allowed to see what you have been working toward. It is not revealed to you, or anyone, beforehand. It takes faith that the "inkling" you received to approach the Lodge door was genuine and heartfelt. It takes spiritual maturity for that to occur.

But it happened to me, and through that work, and becoming a Master Mason myself, was I able to see the private, deep inside life of noble, dedicated, and spiritual men in my community. I was given the gift of their friendship, their counsel, and their confidence. I could see how they managed their lives, and see the whole picture that strict confidentiality allows. I was a part of another group, and was able to see deeper into God's gift of fellowship, compassion and selflessness in people I have come to respect, admire, and depend on.

* * * *

It may sound high-minded, but Rotary's reputation is quickly developing into the de facto standard of compassionate and committed problem-solving around the world. We are demonstrating the power of private, cross-cultural cooperation, communication, and hard work to solve the kind of deep, ugly problems that know no borders. We are showing that we can understand the simple suffering of a parent with a dying child, brothers and sisters existing without hope, and the lament of millions that the more fortunate people just don't care.

For our Club, my sole goal over the last few years has been to increase our ability to solve world problems. My greatest satisfaction is that Roswell East Rotarians can now say with conviction, "No one who comes to us in need, if they have personally dedicated their time and resources to solving some legitimate problem overseas, will be turned away." No one. Every single problem that has been put to us since October, 2005 has been given real, substantial help. How many Rotary Clubs can claim that?

We are becoming far, far more powerful than our

size might indicate. For example, my interest in all things international gave me the energy to achieve funding for humanitarian and Christian missions around the world. I have made many fabulous friends, and been able to help them and their countrymen in need. And I receive credit for doing what I enjoy. That, too, is a gift.

Floro Lavalle and John Jeffrey of the Rotary Club of Pilar, Argentina, have been great friends of mine for years now. We have done a lot of good together, and they have both taught me a thing or two about class, and how to appreciate and enjoy friendship.

Over one hundred years old now, Rotary has come to mean far more to me than it ever could in my youth, and I understand well my father's dedication to it. It brings me closer to him, and what a gift that is! There are so many things I can now understand that I never gave a second thought to before. The world has become far richer, and I far wealthier, than I could have ever imagined.

Chapter Sixteen

The Upward Spiral

Many describe active addiction as an accelerating downward spiral to destruction and death. Once started, it is very difficult to break out of the slide, which can be hidden from the addict by growing denial and fantasy.

In recovery, there is an even more powerful upward spiral of spiritual growth, fueled by increasing clarity and truth. It is based on the enduring rewards of awareness, love, and the grace of a higher power. Tragically, most addicts never break free of the darkness. As one of the few who have, I am humbled in gratitude for the joys and life I have been given. I hope I can be a witness to all those still struggling.

Reversing the downward path requires brokenness. In defeat, we are forced to seek solutions outside of ourselves. We have no more resources; we have nowhere else to turn. The power we need is, by definition, greater than the personal power that has just failed us.

The recognition of a higher power and the acceptance of our limitations create a peace and serenity we may not have felt for some time. For me, it was far greater than anything I had experienced, and was unrelated to events occurring around me.

To continue the upward spiral, I had to follow my curiosity about this new found serenity. That led me to see that this higher power was indeed, God, and I had broken into an entirely new universe of spiritual understanding. This led to more peace, and to greater understanding of God and His providence.

There is danger, however. I have to be conscious that this peace can lead to complacency, which can be deadly to recovery and spiritual growth. Extended complacency, where I might lose the urgency to practice spiritual rituals, can lead to arrogance, pride, and self-seeking behavior. That leads back to brokenness, which is typically more painful than the last. The upward spiral takes work to fend off the downward drift from the gravity of our own self-centeredness.

It takes deliberate action just to stay in one place. It takes even more action to advance, just like any skill.

To me, it is a little depressing to think we are perpetually condemned to continuing decay. That is why I can now understand the "desperation" that motivates many, many very intelligent spiritual leaders. Our goose is basically cooked. But this can be a blessing. It can motivate a humble and rigorous search for God and the willingness to follow directions. That is what led me to grasp God's incredible power to correct my lethal self-destructiveness. I couldn't; He could.

There is a definite kind nature to God, at least in my experience. Only kindness can explain why He gives us feelings such as laughter, awareness, and pure joy itself. Pleasantries in life are not needed for survival, but He gave them to us. Enjoy them! That is true grace. And none of us deserves it, I don't care who you are, or what you have done. I know I don't. I deserve to be dead. But not only am I alive, I am living a dream. My children are growing into wonderful adults before my eyes. My wife is a literal Godsend. We are celebrating twenty-two years of marriage in two weeks, and I wish it could be two hundred more.

I have learned through painful lessons how to tackle and come out on top of many business situations. I have learned how to avoid many problems. I have learned the art of low expectations, in spite of all the rah-rah hype that is taught in training sessions these days. I actually enjoy being a part of the most desperate (when it is not me!) business situations, and squeezing out a solution when the heat is on. Amazingly, people are actually starting to pay me for this! They are asking me to help when the going gets impossible. ME!! And to think I used to be the cause of these types of problems.. You have to be blind not to see God's grace in this and everything else if you stop and really look. I was blind with my eyes wide open for most of my life. Watch out for that; it is very common.

Spiritual growth can be far more constructive than addiction is devastating, which is hard to imagine, but it can. It is well within the category of miracle. Even though it requires work to overcome our natural moral gravity, it can save the most hopeless among us. Addiction's worst case is death. Spiritual growth knows no upper limit. Most people, including me, don't pursue it without the motivation of significant, excruciating pain. But many people do. To them I say congratulations. I admire you and am inspired by your foresight.

The way I have come to know Jesus Christ as my personal Savior has been through the slow, steady dawning of the truth, by my own observation, through an opened mind and curious but critical need to understand reality.

Instead of dismissing my skepticism of God, of Christ, and other religious matters, I embraced it. I needed to know the truth, however the chips may fall. And my way of discovering truth is through rigorous examination, without pre-judgment. Truth has a tendency to weather scrutiny where fantasy and denial cannot. I never thought Christianity could withstand such observation, but I had never put it to the test. Frankly, it was too much work. And for most of my life, I thought I knew all the answers. So there was no real need to bother. But closing my mind to the possibility of religious truth, at the wizened age of thirteen, I had never examined spiritual matters for myself, on my terms, according to my criteria of truth. Now, as a father in my 50's, I need to know the truth. Life is harder than in my teens.

I have reached a point in my life where I have no time for fantasies. I am not going to speculate about things where I might be wrong, because I can no longer afford to be wrong. I am a father of three children, and I am rebuilding a business from scratch, under difficult circumstances. I have a lot to be grateful for, but I have also been given responsibility that, so far, I have been able to handle. The growth required has been very uncomfortable at times, and I would not do it if I did not have to. But I do.

In this war of rebuilding the finances I destroyed, I have no time and no room to be frivolous, or childish, or naïve, about where the solution to my worldly problems will come from. I have to accept what is. In fact, I not only have to accept it, I have to seek truth and find it. I am forced, through pain and adversity, to find anything that can help me manage and get past the problems of today.

Pain is quite motivating like that.

Knowing that my business problems were way beyond my lowly abilities to overcome, I kept searching for whatever it was that produced the miracle of my sobriety. I knew for certain that 1) it was not me that got me clean and 2) I couldn't risk being wrong. I didn't have the luxury of time. My family had to be fed, housed, educated, and raised.

But I had the experience of recovery. When the "ox was in the ditch", when I *had* to succeed, I was able to do so by humble prayer, acceptance, and submission to my higher power.

So what was this "higher power"? Thinking about it, the concept was very bizarre. Some ethereal power we can't see controls everything and personally seeks a relationship with us? Once I scoffed at this as mere mythology of the childish, but I had evidence, living, breathing evidence. It is everywhere. Nowhere was it more rewarding than the positive transformation in the lives of my wife, my children, my parents, and in my friends.

The more I thought about, observed, experienced, and studied this power, a vague image slowly emerged from a haze of clouds and static. More visceral than visual, imagine a static-filled television screen with no reception. Slowly, a vague shape starts to appear, or voices just out of earshot, where you hear talking that is too soft to understand the words.

With regular spiritual maintenance, study, and open-minded searching for the true nature of things, this shape began to take on the form of this thing called God I have been hearing so much about.

It started to fit.

This is what millions of people have discovered

before me! What an idiot I've been! How could I miss something that has been surrounding me all my life? Better yet, there was a mountain range of material, discussion, and discoveries people have been generating about God for centuries.

The first was the Bible itself. Soon after I began my re-energized quest, I participated in many God-related discussions. I found out quickly how little I knew. I had never bothered to study these matters. My ego had kidnapped my intellect, and now I was discovering the depth of my ignorance. One friend suggested simply that I read the Bible. It had been an incredible experience for him.

So I did, over the course of a year. What I discovered was amazing and unexpected. The Bible was different from what I had been told about all these years. It was much easier to understand. I found an incredible amount of historical facts, sources of many modern sayings, and the foundations of many prominent public documents. I also noticed a certain timelessness about the lessons illustrated in this ancient text. The problems people had then are the same as we have today, as are most of the solutions. No wonder this is the all time best-seller. I was even more intrigued.

By the time I reached the New Testament, I was in a weekly Bible Study with a great group of people who were kind enough to show me how to study the Bible seriously.

They also showed me how they had found Truth when they, too, couldn't afford to kid themselves. They all supported families, had responsible jobs, and had to manage their lives just like me. Life is hard enough, but living in a dream is impossible. These people knew this and had discovered that the search for God's truth helped them live a life worth living. You cannot help others if you are in a self-concocted fantasy, and helping others is the surest way of helping yourself. Odd, but true.

Slowly I began to understand the Holy Spirit, since it was growing in me. Not only did I have this sense of peace and serenity that by all rights I shouldn't have, but I had both an energy and an instinct to help others that was completely out of character, at least for the sleazy, jerk that had occupied my brain the fifteen years or so before I got clean.

Finally, I began to see how Jesus fit into the picture, into the Trinity to be exact. This was as humbling as it was magnificent. I had come full circle, and was now one baby-step through a doorway that had been open to me all of my life. What had taken me so long? A very thick skull, that's what. God knew I had to be taught every lesson thoroughly before the message sunk in.

For now, I am just looking out for those little messages God sends me when he wants me to do something. Those big messages are just too painful to take, but if I don't take heed of the small ones, the bigger ones

always follow, and remind me that the joys of an upward
spiral require work, diligence, and gratitude.

Chapter Seventeen

Peace in Reality

More and more, the world seems to be dishing out a relentless amount of stress on all of us. We hear about road rage, employment insecurity, bestsellers of gloom, and innumerable accounts of antidotes for depression and anxiety.

There seems to be a collective yearning for tranquility, and in advertising, serenity sells. It doesn't sell like sex or vanity, but it sells. We all want peace.

Almost everyone that follows the spiritual principles we have outlined thus far can be rewarded with a peace and serenity they have never known. It just takes action.

This peace is not deserved, and it is not due to the days' events. I have felt it, even during my most stressful and anxious times. In fact, as I write this, I have been increasingly anxious about the inability to visualize how I will solve a few knotty problems. Since these problems recur, I should know better. I should realize that I am never going to precisely know the way things will turn out, and beating myself up for answers is destructive. Somehow, though, my conscience won't let me completely relax. Not worrying is too similar to sleeping on the job. Thankfully, scripture gives guidance:

> *"be anxious about nothing, but in everything by prayer and supplication with thanksgiving let your requests be made known to God. And the peace of God, which surpasses all understanding, will guard your hearts and your minds in Christ Jesus."*
>
> *Philippians 4:6-7*

I am taught to have faith in the Father and let Him handle the problems. So I pray. I do a quick spiritual, mental, and physical checklist:

1) Have I been eating well?
2) Have I had enough sleep?
3) Have I been running/exercising in the last two days?
4) Have I been praying diligently?
5) Have I been to a recovery meeting lately?
6) Have I told my wife and children and Dad that I love them?

7)   Have I stopped to recognize all the blessings
        in my life, and how many billions of people
        on Earth would happily trade their problems
        for mine?

Usually, I find one or more of these items amiss. Even
before I bring all of these current, I feel better.

The peace I have found since becoming clean is a
result of living a spiritual life. It is not constant though, and
I have to work at maintaining my spiritual condition.

Recovery literature promises us a "peace we have
never known", if we adhere to the program. This is quite
true, and is a miracle in itself. However, as I began studying
more and more with my newly opened mind, my curiosity
and respect enabled me to see that this peace was far larger,
far grander, and had a far deeper background than I had
imagined.

In my second or third year of recovery, I was
interacting with more and more spiritual people of varied
backgrounds who had come to their beliefs and faith
through many different avenues, not just from addiction.

I slowly became aware that I was experiencing a
phenomenon that was known to millions, and had been
discussed widely for thousands of years. Is it possible to live
forty active years on this planet and completely miss this?
Knowing my complete lack of curiosity in some areas, I
guess it is. All this time I have considered myself a very

aware and observant student of the world. Worldly, in fact. But I was nowhere near as wise as my ego told me I was. It is humbling to realize just how small and how unaware we can be.

Sam Anders, after-care chief at Ridgeview Institute, has seen a lot of addicts. He was fifteen years sober himself when I met him, and I didn't like him. I had been imprisoned in that psychiatric hospital for five weeks when he told me my lack of progress felt to him like I was committing suicide. I was furious. How could he say that to me? I thought I deserved a lot more respect that he gave me. To him, I was just another arrogant addict that was fighting recovery versus embracing it. He was right, too. He predicted we could all obtain a serenity we had never known if we followed certain steps. In my denial, I thought he was nuts.

Have you ever thought of contentment as a cop-out for those who can't compete? Is contentment weakness? Is it a sign of laziness? Isn't it noble to make your own way in the world, overcoming obstacles, and needing no one?

Success and achievement, within God's will, produce serenity. Complacency, which is easily confused with contentment, pulls us away for His will, and leads us to inaction. In doing so, it can doom our ultimate success.

As my spiritual side developed, while working the first ten steps, I became ready for an even greater concept. This is the eleventh of the "twelve steps", and has come to me to embody all of the New Testament, and a whole lot of Old:

> *"Sought through prayer and meditation to improve my conscious contact with God, as I understand him, praying only for the knowledge of His Will for me, and the power to carry it out."*

When I can corral my mind to this concept, I realize it is all we really need. Everything we will ever do in the future falls under the vast umbrella of this simple, short, life-changing notion.

Once you have given your life to God, you no longer have to watch over your shoulder, or your rear view mirror, for that great, unknown catastrophe waiting to confirm your self-centered paranoia. We should revel in the fact that the world doesn't care what we do. We are not that important to others. Relax. Nobody cares what we do unless it creates paperwork.

A good relationship with God, looking to Him for our needs, guidance, and affirmation, takes a lot of pressure off our relationships with others. I have been able to enjoy the fellowship of other Christians who are more like me than I ever imagined. Laugh about difficulties. Enjoy with others the common relationship with God. We all struggle to do right, despite human flaws that will never allow us to succeed perfectly. Bond with friends, acknowledge your fallibilities, and do not take yourself too seriously. Laugh at yourself out loud, and be grateful for the world, the friends, the family, and the heart God gave you. Breathe. Sleep. Eat. Exercise. Read scripture often. Be conscious of your human frailties, but be comforted knowing that the guidance the Lord gives through His Son and His scripture insures that we can always return to His path when we stray.

* * * *

Another source of peace comes from knowing that you do not have to react to everything and everyone. Most of the world will go on without our intervention, if we can accept this humbling truth.

For a long time I was plagued by excessive anxiety, earmarked by panic attacks, fear of flying, and that feeling that things were spinning out of control. In my twenties, I developed a huge fear of bridges. It was a combination of a fear of heights and loss of control. I would panic when going over a bridge, the thinner and higher the worse. Sometimes I would cower on the floor, on the passenger side of the car, not even being able to ride over them.

This expanded to a general fear of heights, especially in airplanes, where there is no escape for hours. Of course, the operative antidote was always cocktails, many of them. They had that wonderfully reliable cause and effect that chemicals do so well. Drink a double scotch, remove cowardice and fear. Drink another double, feel like a king. Drink another, everyone's a king!

What we don't realize is that alcohol and drugs, while relieving our fears in the short term, do just the opposite in the long term, especially when taken in excess over long periods of time. While alcohol will calm you in a hurry, it can rip your nervous system to shreds. The massive doses of artificially engineered emotion prevent the body from dealing with fear, threats, and resentments in a healthy way. Indirectly, the late nights, the hangovers, no exercise, the bad eating, the bizarre sleep habits, the worry, the smoking, the increased likelihood of drug use, and drunk driving do little to strengthen ones nerves and demeanor.

The greatest technique to obtain peace, in my sober experience, is the grateful acceptance of reality and the dependence on God and others to show you things you can't learn for yourself.

Reality takes getting used to. Most of us are in the habit of avoiding it, twisting it, hiding from it, or pretending it will go away. Our minds are built to accommodate our perceptions, and our perceptions can be extremely subjective. By isolating ourselves from the world, we can protect the bubble of fantasy we create. The more we are alone, the more our minds can reinforce our denial and false assumptions. Frequently it is our ego, hurt by fact or shame, and yearning for some relief from the truth, that spawns justifications, rationalizations, and resentments.

I was in Florida a few years ago, about a six hour drive from my home in Atlanta. Having finished my business, I wanted to stay another night, maybe play some golf, or just relax in the good weather. My wife had other ideas. She had been tending to the demands of our three active, outgoing kids for more than a few days, and needed me at home. She was exhausted, as it is always hard on one parent when the other is away, and all of the house and family responsibilities are left on their shoulders.

She was a bit sarcastic concerning my motives for wanting to stay in Florida, as she was counting on me coming home and helping out with the house and children. I didn't like it, but I grumbled to myself, got in my car, and started back to Atlanta. Just like a good little boy.

It wasn't that big of a deal. It certainly wasn't when I started back. Just a little disagreement, nothing more.

After all, she was right, I acknowledged, even though I couldn't quite envision her predicament. But a six hour drive is a long time to spend with my most dangerous company, me. A car can be like a sealed Petri dish of mental obsession, a capsule of my own kingdom that for short bursts can protect my denial and let my ego warp any perception that does not fit its view.

What began as a mild irritation on my part began to grow into something else. As the hours rolled by, the more I

WITNESS 195

came to believe that I deserved a few days in Florida, and that she was being selfish. With no one or anything to interfere, my ego kept hammering at what a great guy I was, how fair I was, and how noble I was to drive all that way to accommodate my wife. More hours passed and this internal conversation continued to build. By the time I arrived at home, my unchecked ego had built up a huge resentment at her taking advantage of my good nature, and of talking to me in a way that did not show the proper respect for a man of my stature. I kid you not.

I entered the front door, tired from the trip, hungry, and irritable. They say this is usually not a good time to unload on your wife (who was also tired, irritable, and waiting for a break), and they are right! Well, I was so wrapped up in my own way of seeing things that I didn't care. What I had to say simply needed to be said. She needed to be corrected.

Emily had forgotten about it, and welcomed me home graciously, warmly, and with love. I started out with "Hold on just a minute, hon, we need to talk." and proceeded to get it off my chest. Bad move.

Well, it was I who ended up apologizing later that night, begging forgiveness for having upbraided her for even thinking she could be so selfish. I was being selfish. Even though no facts changed in the six hours of that drive, my perception of the facts changed wildly, enough to put me in hot water with someone I love and know well. It quickly became clear to me that I had contrived almost all of it in my head, and ruined what should have been a marvelous homecoming with my need to be right.

It is so easy to do. You would think I would have seen it happening. I had been clean for some years, and I had paid a lot of attention to spiritual principles. But the mind and the ego are powerful protectors of themselves, and I see a lot of suffering every day because of it.

We need to deal with reality. Everyday, no matter how much we avoid it, there it is. We can only control a mere fraction of it, far less than our egos say we can. If we can do so little in a harsh and cruel world, why aren't we paralyzed with fear? Because we can adapt and we can learn to manage our lives in such a way that God will let even the least deserving of us live. Even flourish. But the world can be cruel, and everyone gets their comeuppance sometime.

The good news is that we can change. We can adapt to the uncertainties reality continually presents, and even develop a little confidence, self-esteem, even style, in dealing with real life with the help and power of God. And it takes the power of God to do it. Our human side is always eroding our spiritual side, so we need to actively practice a program to maintain ourselves in reality.

Our self-absorption sometimes shows up as a paranoid-like concern where we need to watch our every move. The truth is that no one is really after us, because they really don't care. That is hard for the ego to swallow, but think about it. Are we concerned at all about what our neighbors are doing at this very moment? How much do we think about ourselves versus other people? Probably a thousand to one! Those few people we do think about are usually those that can give us something. Unless a stranger just happens to amuse us, they are nothing but wallpaper in our world.

When we shift our perspective from ourselves to God, there is a clearing of the mind that can be scary. Our perspective is a hazy tunnel vision, from one infinitesimal point in the universe, warped by emotions and corrupted by ego, that excludes far more information than it includes. God's perspective is clear, unemotional, accepting, and encompasses all. It is truth, and it is confirmed as truth over time.

If people are telling you something you disagree with over and over again, they might be right. If science confirms certain facts again and again, they might be true. If you keep getting drunk and getting in trouble, you might just be an alcoholic. If you mow your lawn and keep finding cars, you might be a redneck, no matter how sophisticated and urbane your new doublewide. (Thanks, Jeff Foxworthy).

So what does this have to do with "Peace"?

Anxiety is produced from fear, and there is no bigger fear than that of the unknown. The more you depend on your own perceptions and try to control the world yourself, or believe things you cannot control should act a certain way, the more you need to worry. History will have shown you that. The more you base your world on denial and ego, the more you are going to have reality correct those perceptions, usually jarring you back into the real world.

With the acceptance of reality, with frequent prayer to God to open and clear your mind, with increased knowledge of how small and warped our senses are, and how much there is still left to learn, there is a paradoxical peace that comes from knowing you are clearing away subjective, emotional fantasy, for the granite of enduring truth. Solid, true, recurring affirmations, confirmed by others who have experienced the same spiritual enlightenment, are what provide a reliable path to reality, that stays steadfast for all who seek it. Not only have we been given the loving fellowship of those who have gone before us, we have been given a guidebook that has remained unaltered and perfectly applicable for over 2000 years.

If all of that is too difficult, or too long, or our ego will not allow it, we are told simply to remember to 1) "Love the Lord your God with all your heart, with all of your mind, and with all of your soul", and 2) "Love your neighbor as yourself". Do these two things well, we are told, and you will go a long way in dealing with the reality of the universe, even if you cannot fully understand or comprehend it now. You can have peace now. Accept reality. Don't be swayed by its harshness, its gentleness, its simplicity, or its vast unknown complexity; it simply is.

* * * *

Accepting reality is a high form of honesty. It is an important spiritual honesty that goes far beyond our dealings with others. It is the honesty within ourselves, and it is far harder than simply not stealing, or even not deceiving. It is the honesty of being able to look at ourselves from the outside, as a stranger might, with no judgments or emotion or ego, just absorbing the facts about you objectively.

Doing this takes practice. I have to practice spiritual principles on an ongoing basis in order to see from outside myself. From my mind's eye, I try to look at myself as someone would high in the sky, watching me sit in traffic, or working, or shopping, or pondering how different I am when I am no different at all. Maybe there are hundreds or thousands of people like me doing, thinking, and feeling the same thing. Some choose to behave in a way that makes future life easier, taking actions now that will pay off later on. When I manage to do this, based on a foundation of truth, I realize that the actions I take in the next few hours are the only parts of my future that I can supply. When I am honest in my dealings with reality, sometimes even having those perceptions verified by others more aware than me, I am given a serenity and peace that lasts.

This peace is far more than what was promised to me by Sam Anders in rehab ten years ago. Having that peace now, and by sharing my journey, I can do my part to show others. It is available to us all.

"God, grant me the serenity to accept the things I cannot change, the courage to change the things I can, and the wisdom to know the difference."

The Serenity Prayer

Chapter Eighteen

Helping Others

Helping others is what God wants us to do. At first, it may seem unnatural, even counter-intuitive. It is against our animal self-centeredness. It's also the path to great and quick reward, spiritual and practical.

If I receive nothing more from God's grace, I will consider my children to be the greatest gift He has given me. Early in my family's life, my children were an afterthought, an adornment to my self-inflated estate. I was so shallow, and so naïve, I had not begun to fathom the thousands of trials and heartbreaks besetting the average parent. My childish eyes could not see the pain and hurt and desperation in my wife, whose clearer head saw the damage an alcoholic father was doing, and would continue to do, to the childhoods of kids.

Addiction recovery meetings are filled with children of these tragic environments. One reason addiction runs in families is that the dysfunctional childhood environment of fear, chaos, insecurity, and loveless inattention plants roots of mental anguish that aren't easily corrected. Fertilized by a life filled with intimidating challenges and terrors that children are never taught to deal with adequately, substance abuse and anti-social, self-destructive ways of coping become habit. Once the behavior is imbedded, it is hard to overcome.

I speak from my personal experience here, but I do realize that my behaviors, which I thought at the time were perfectly normal and respectable, were actually pathological impersonations of what I thought a parent should be like. Was I wrong!

From my many interactions with other parents, I know that such insincerity is crippling to a child. Since a child looks largely to a parent first to form conclusions about the realities of the world, and because children have such an uncanny antennae for insincerity, it's hard to raise a well balanced child where there is little reality. This is especially true when the parent lives his life as a child, pinning hopes on fantasy and treating the world with an arrogant disdain that only serves to antagonize it. It is hard enough to raise children being the most honest and forthright person on earth. Dishonesty only compounds the probability of social problems later on. Perhaps it is the result of my wonderful wife's desperate prayer while I was lost to an evil oblivion, and it is certainly nothing I actively did in the least, but my three children are all beautiful, healthy growing young adults that I thank God and my wife for every day. What a gift!

In my last year of active addiction, my oldest son, John, was nine years old. We had quite a close relationship, but from age four or five on, he began to show the adverse social effects of a father in self-absorbed self-destruction.

I was a smart-aleck. So he began to see the world in this way also. Since I had a brief flurry of business success, I developed into quite an arrogant cynic. I often pointed out to my son all of the idiots around us who didn't have the world by the string as well as I did. Never having had wealth, I rather enjoyed the luxury of looking down on everyone. It was juvenile, but fun. Add drugs and alcohol, with their gasoline like ability to fuel ego and self-inflation, and the inferno of ego exploded. Self-centeredness gone wild.

My son caught on to the big laugh I was having at the world, and learned to join in the fun. Unbeknownst to my blind eyes, his attitude began causing social problems his mother and doctors saw but were helpless to contain. Of course, their reasoning was met by my dismissing disdain.

When a parent, and through them a child, stops having respect for others and for those that truly care for them, relationships suffer. What better way to snuff out budding friendships, or to eviscerate personal relationships than to disrespect those around you? My child was not developing socially, and the withdrawn behavior was a direct result of my attitude and behavior. Everyone knew it but me.

I know it now. How?

Because of God's grace, my life in recovery has had a miraculous effect on the mental and spiritual maturity of my children. Even if I had never taught them any specific lesson, their witness to God's work in me and our household, taught them much. They saw me pray on my knees every morning. Here was this big adult who had to beg for God's grace and forgiveness for one more day clean. I had to be willing, and God was able to pass through me to guide my actions and my decisions, and take up residence to benefit the lives of my children.

If you aren't a parent, you may never know what a gift that is, or the gratitude a human can be capable of, but it is humbling to receive and humbling to witness. God is real and alive, and will take care of all of us if we allow Him. Praise God.

Beyond our children, the effect of taking the spiritual road can spell renewed energy and good will toward our spouses, friends, parents, and others.

When I first began recovery, I was told to serve others in order to help myself. I didn't understand that at all. Most of the time, addicts enter sobriety at their lowest possible point on the spiritual spectrum. I think this is a prime reason so many addicts don't make it out of active addiction. Getting off drugs is one of the most spiritually demanding exercises that comes at a time when one is the weakest. Looking back after ten years, and seeing the process by which my recovery unfolded, it is almost impossible to see the path before the fact. Many times, people have actually tried recovery and failed, so the imprint of a painful path of self-denial leading only to tragedy and hopelessness is implanted.

Active addiction itself tends to drive you to a hyper, self-centered, immediate gratification way of dealing with the world, where the only seemingly reliable cause-effect relationship is chemical. You snort it, you feel better. You run out, you get more, you feel better. No snort, you feel worse.

This process is pounded into an addict's head to the point where it is nearly impossible to reverse. Only "right now" matters. Planning is impossible. Doing something painful today, to be better off tomorrow, is way too complex for an addict. Addiction reverses maturity. It beats it back into childhood, even infancy in extreme cases.

After a few years sober, I attended a meeting in the lock-down detox unit of Ridgeview. Most of the patients had just come off the streets. Detox is always the first stop in any rehab process. It is a highly staffed, tightly secured, closed facility where intoxicated new patients are typically brought for their first few days to get the drugs out of their system. Patients can be violent, overdosed, have medical emergencies, delusions, psychopathic episodes–literally anything. Straight jackets and restraints are always kept nearby.

Most people in the meeting had only a few days off drugs and/or alcohol. They did not look good. One fellow, who was visiting from the outside and had been sober enough to put a few words together, looked normal in your typical sense of the word. Tall, fit, clean pressed jeans and shirt, well groomed hair, sensible demeanor.

He began to relay a little story about why he was there.

Not long before, he'd been drinking two bottles of vodka a day, and no one could tell him anything to help him. He quit driving, and was fired from his job. He holed up in his house all day, drinking whatever he could find. When he ran out of booze, he would drink mouthwash (Scope, for example, is thirty percent alcohol). He didn't care. He had to have it. During one drunk, he fell and broke an arm, then fell again and broke the other arm. Another time, he could only tip his bottle into a dog bowl and lapped it up. Still another time, he vomited on his dirty kitchen floor so he could lap up the undigested remnants of the bottle he drank earlier in the day.

He said he should be dead. But "by the grace of God and recovery" he was alive today. And sober. He cared enough to come back to the detox unit, the last hope for the hopeless, and encourage those who thought there is no solution, no life except jails, institutions, and death, to surrender to a program of recovery that can and does work miracles for thousands.

It is the generosity of such recovering addicts that is so critical to passing on the unfathomable gift of life to addicts seeking a new way to live. For me, such people gave me enough hope to take another step, another minute, another day. They were clean, sober, serene, happy, and generally funny. There is something special about recovering addicts, especially to each other. Perhaps it's because they have pretty much endured everything, and have probably encountered every comical situation known to man. There is nothing bad you have ever done that cannot be topped by someone else in a room of recovering addicts. For some reason, there is security in that.

I try to be that person to others entering the program. I try to be as open as my midget mind will let me, and tell everyone who will listen what happened to me, no matter how embarrassing, so that they might share their pain and problems with me or others, and not miss solutions others have found. No matter what we go through in life, someone has been through it, and there is a way to manage.

My service life has expanded greatly, but God seems to make things happen that provide me the time and money to do what He wants. Not only has he shown the path to service as a husband, father, friend, Christian, Mason, and now Stephen Minister, he has also given me Rotary International as a fun and exciting vehicle to do His work in a secular environment.

My father is a Rotarian, but I never paid it much mind until I was in recovery a few years. It always seemed too rigid and organized for a free spirit such as myself. Ha! My parents had a lot of exchange students stay in our home over the years, and a few of them, thirty-five years later, are some of my closest friends in the world.

Those early fellowships with people from other countries have given me a never ending fascination with the world and other cultures. Once I spent my sophomore college year in the great city of London. I was hooked. However, all of that youthful enthusiasm seemed to die away over the years, until I re-involved myself in Rotary. I had no idea what Rotary would mean to me as an adult in recovery. But I committed anyway, even though I could not see the payoff (sound familiar by now?). Soon after I joined, I was asked to be on the International Projects committee, which was responsible for arranging grant monies for humanitarian efforts outside the U.S. To me, I was amazed that the biggest problem was that no one knew how to find the people who needed the money! I realized what a great opportunity this would be to help my friends. If I could learn to obtain grant money for people who desperately needed it, I would have done something big. Really big.

Not many Rotarians have the patience to serve this

function well. One has to understand the culture and problems in developing countries and how to manage around them. Since I had some experience in this area, the problems that often vexed others were not discouraging to me. I also knew in advance what an incredible difference this money would make, so I was willing to persevere. Most important was the commitment to see things to the end, even if I had to slow down, or set things aside for a while. Others depended on me to keep the ball rolling.

We have had an incredible amount of success in just a few short years.

In engineering a partnership between my church and Rotary International, we funded a community kitchen and children's center in the drug-torn border town of Nuevo Laredo, Mexico. In a poor, dusty barrio outside of town, a small Methodist Church had been struggling for years. Its prayerful pastor, Valeriano Garcia, had been slowly building a church and a safe gathering place for the many children and adults. Their houses were mere hovels without water or electricity.

Given a few parched acres next to this barrio, Pastor Vale first raised funds to build a fence around the land. This area lies directly on the path where a steady stream of poor migrants travel from even poorer regions of Central America and Southern Mexico.

If you gaze through the blowing dust across the landscape littered with decrepit shacks and trash, you see a giant American flag flying just on the other side of the border. It is a moving contrast to witness.

Within the fence, Pastor Vale built a small church and then a playground. He had made tireless and expensive trips to U.S. churches to inspire support. Slowly, his prayers and efforts were rewarded, and out of the hard clay rose up a safe place for the children and a small well of hope for the families.

Regular mission trips and donations followed. The little church built a crude fellowship hall out of concrete blocks. Most of the labor was donated by mission teams from the U.S., particularly here in Georgia. Roswell United Methodist Church (RUMC) and Johns Creek Methodist have taken the lead in supporting the Mexican church, named Inglesia Metodista de Nuevo Pacto. There were walls and a roof, but nothing inside.

Soon the violence escalated so that no mission teams could safely visit. Pastor Vale's dream slipped away. They redoubled their prayers and their faith.

Somehow, I felt it.

I had met Pastor Vale at a conference at my Roswell church, about the time the drug violence was shutting down most of the official mission trips. By this time, I already had a few years experience with Rotary's matching grant programs. I heard his story and got an inkling, entirely from God, that I could combine Rotary's humanitarian goals with this effort, add in a little know-how, and get Pastor

Vale's kitchen built. We did just that.

As part of the grant requirements, I had to find a Mexican Rotary Club that was willing to assist us in the project. Rotary's goals are to stimulate cross-cultural cooperation between Rotarians of various countries, as well as humanitarian relief. To fund a project, they require that two Rotary clubs, of different nationalities, work together.

Introducing myself to the Rotary Club of Nuevo Laredo, I found a most gracious, generous, and compassionate group of businessmen. They had great hearts for their community and knew it was under siege. They were desperate as the dark side was overrunning Nuevo Laredo. Their own members were being kidnapped for ransom just for being Rotarians.

Through their mighty efforts, particularly past President Luis Zamudio, and President Luis Benetiz Perez, we not only built Pastor Vale's kitchen, we put in motion a second project to provide clean, healthy water to the poor in Nuevo Laredo. The Nuevo Laredo Rotarians were moved by the fact that a stranger from a foreign country, with no other connection than a shared sense of humanity, had concern for them and their community.

They felt they needed to do something for *our* community of Roswell. They sponsored a new matching grant to provide desperately needed funds for the Drakehouse, a women and children's shelter here in Roswell, Georgia. This is one of the first Rotary matching grants *ever* to originate in Latin America to benefit a community in the U.S. The rewards of my little effort have been incredible.

We have been blessed with success in many other parts of the world. In Argentina, we were able to screen thousands of public school children for vision problems, and provide free eyeglasses and corrective surgery as needed. In many developing countries, if a child cannot read well, there is no one to identify the problem as a simple want of glasses or minor surgery. Tragically, the education is all too often halted, and thousands of otherwise productive lives are derailed into government or private dependency.

With the tireless operational oversight of the Rotary Club of Pilar, Argentina, we were able to recruit hundreds of local doctors, school teachers, and parents to accomplish this great task. Now, there will be no tragic loss of education for those who have been born with what most of the world considers a minor problem. Twenty years from now, no one will see that blind beggar on the street that would have been there if we had not acted. No one will even wonder why, or who was responsible. That's okay. All of us involved know that future parents will not have to watch their child grow up uneducated, or permanently dependent. No one will have to look at any of these thousands of children and say "it is a shame someone didn't do anything". Someone did do something. With the help of God, we did.

Not only do these efforts demonstrate how to bring

out the best in people, no matter the country, no matter the language, it allows all of our children to grow up productive, educated, and prepared to contribute. Their community is better; mankind is better.

We are on our fifth grant project in Argentina, our third in Mexico. While great fun personally, it is also a deep comfort to know that someone like me, with my self-obsessed history, could even be interested in something like this, much less invigorated!

There are many satisfactions, but there is one honor that stands particularly high. That is to experience fellow parents, frequently from a foreign country, tearfully thanking me for saving the life of their child. Living my former life, I would have never heard these words. If anything, my reckless behavior could have resulted in the death of someone's child. Left to my own devices, I had the shame, guilt, and wrath of those around me. Now I have far more than just the absence of these dangers. I have honor, respect, and the deep serenity that doing for others brings me more than I could ever do by my own design.

Helping others is the only sure way of helping yourself. When you need a lot of help, when matters look particularly difficult, try to remember this truth.

For me, the solution always comes back to the God I was shown as a child, but ignored for so many years. I can only improve my ability to see what he plans for me, and do it. I can never do it perfectly. I am not that smart. I am an imperfect, self-serving human that does not deserve the grace I have received. But I have received it, and for the sake of my family, my friends, my own continued spiritual growth, and all those in the world fighting for a better way to live, I make my decision to turn my will and my life to He who reigns over all.

Chapter Nineteen

Thank you

Thank you, reader, for your time. As we both step into the future, I hope you will find my experiences and observations useful. If my only purpose in life is to "serve as a warning to others", I hope I have carried the message clearly. Keep in touch. My email address is lee@leehollingsworth.com. Please let me hear from you. There is much to do, and much to share. There is no need to bear your cross alone.

We must learn from each other, and lift each other up. *"Finally, brethren, whatsoever things are true, whatsoever things are honest, whatsoever things are just, whatsoever things are pure, whatsoever things are lovely, whatsoever things are of good report; if there be any virtue, and if there be any praise, think on these things. Those things, which ye have both learned, and received, and heard, and seen in me, do: and the God of peace shall be with you. "*

Philippians 4: 8,9

ACKNOWLEDGEMENTS

Though a woefully incomplete list, the following people deserve my deep gratitude and acknowledgement of their role in this project. God truly works through them.

Emily Hollingsworth

Marjorie Joyner Hollingsworth

Florence "Sister" Sheffield

Wright Hollingsworth

Pat Worley

Lorraine Hollingsworth Dajani

Virginia Arthur

Mike Hollingsworth

Margaret Hollingsworth

William Wright

W.E.B. Griffin

Judy Walker

Nancy Folsom Lane

Paula Krzyzaniak

Sam Anders

Howard Hunter

Lori & PJ Teza

John, Katherine, and Langdon Hollingsworth

Joe & Carla Martin

Lewis Hunter

Lance Hunter

Guillermo Gonzalez-Prieto

John Jeffrey

Floro Lavalle

Langdon Sheffield

Trish & Jim Sheffield

Pete Sheffield

Jack Brown

Rick Hull

In addition, I need to thank the thousands of people I have met in recovery, whose strength and love have been my salvation. I will never know most of their names. I can never repay them, but I can give away what they freely gave me. This book is part of that effort.

APPENDIX

The Twelve Steps
Narcotics Anonymous Version

1. We admitted that we were powerless over our addiction, that our lives had become unmanageable.

2. We came to believe that a Power greater than ourselves could restore us to sanity.

3. We made a decision to turn our will and our lives over to the care of God as we understood Him.

4. We made a searching and fearless moral inventory of ourselves.

5. We admitted to God, to ourselves, and to another human being the exact nature of our wrongs.

6. We were entirely ready to have God remove all these defects of character.

7. We humbly asked Him to remove our
   shortcomings.

8. We made a list of all persons we had harmed, and
   became willing to make amends to them all.

9. We made direct amends to such people wherever
   possible, except when to do so would injure
   them or others.

10. We continued to take personal inventory and
    when we were wrong promptly admitted it.

11. We sought through prayer and meditation to
    improve our conscious contact with God as
    we understood Him, praying only for
    knowledge of His will for us and the power
    to carry that out.

12. Having had a spiritual awakening as a result of
    these steps, we tried to carry this message
    to addicts, and to practice these principles
    in all our affairs.